Writing to Inform and Persuade

BY CAROLYN KANE, Ph.D.

COPYRIGHT © 1997 Mark Twain Media, Inc.

Printing No. CD–1862

Mark Twain Media, Inc., Publishers
Distributed by Carson-Dellosa Publishing Company, Inc.

TABLE OF CONTENTS

PART FIVE: Propaganda

PART SIX: The Creative Process

TO THE TEACHER

This activity book deals with informative and argumentative writing, logic, and the creative process. It is a sequel to *Grammar and Composition,* which covered the construction of sentences and included a unit on the paragraph and the short essay. *Writing to Inform and Persuade* begins with a brief introduction to rhetoric and continues with further practice in essay-writing. Written assignments cover most of the familiar rhetorical types—narration, description, exemplification, definition, classification, and cause-and-effect reasoning—but not the process essay and the essay of comparison/contrast, which were included in *Grammar and Composition.*

The units that follow deal with persuasion, logic, propaganda, and creative thinking. These chapters include a number of short writing projects, as well as the major assignment of a persuasive essay. As the students work through the book, the teacher might find it useful to let them hold discussions and performances—to present their arguments in favor of mayoral candidates Ms. Yapp and Mr. Zilch (page 22), or to display their salesmanship by pitching Fizzle Cola and Cloud Nine Sportswear to the class (page 62), or to hold a mock election for student council (page 44). If the students enjoy using their imaginations and displaying their theatrical talents, they might also discover that thinking does not have to be dreary and tedious, and that using the mind can be fun.

This book is affectionately dedicated to Sharon Upchurch, Librarian of Culver-Stockton College, with gratitude for years of friendship and support.

—THE AUTHOR

FURTHER READING

Many books and articles are available for people who want to learn more about rhetoric, logic, and the art of writing. Most publishers of college-level textbooks offer at least one good book on rhetoric, and many of these books contain excellent essays as examples of the different rhetorical purposes and strategies. A good writer's handbook will often include a section on logic and logical fallacies. For anyone who wants to write in a clear and readable style, the classic textbook is a short work entitled *The Elements of Style,* by William Strunk and E.B. White. William Zinsser's *On Writing Well* is also helpful.

For further reading on the manipulation and misuse of language, a good starting point is George Orwell's classic essay, "Politics and the English Language." Carl Sagan's book *The Demon-Haunted World* contains a discussion of logical fallacies in a chapter entitled "The Fine Art of Baloney Detection." A classic work on statistical manipulation is *How to Lie with Statistics,* by Darrell Huff. Carl P. Wrighter's book, *I Can Sell You Anything,* contains some useful examples of weasel words.

Finally, if you would like to learn more about quackery through the ages, read Martin Gardner's amusing and readable book, *Fads and Fallacies in the Name of Science.* For further illustrations, see the section entitled "The Paradoxers" in Carl Sagan's *Brocca's Brain.*

INTRODUCTION

What is Rhetoric?

This book is an introduction to the art of writing effectively and persuasively. Scholars and teachers call this **rhetoric** (RET-ur-ik). Rhetoric is an old study: people have been teaching it and learning about it for centuries. Over 2,000 years ago, the Greek teacher and philosopher, Aristotle (AIR-iss-tah-tuhl), compiled his lecture notes into a book about how to write and speak convincingly. He did this job so thoroughly and so well that his book, *Rhetoric,* is still considered one of the best works on the art of communication. But Aristotle is by no means the only authority: every year a typical English teacher can expect to receive a stack of advertisements from publishers offering to sell the newest, most improved books about rhetoric.

But why, one might ask, should Aristotle or anyone else go to the trouble of writing a thick book about how to use language? After all, doesn't language come naturally to human beings? If so, why don't we just write what is in our hearts? Why don't we simply say what we mean in the most honest and sincere words that come to mind? Unfortunately, good communication is neither easy nor simple—as you know if you have ever tried to win an argument with a friend or if you have ever stared at a piece of blank paper and tried desperately to think of an idea for a school assignment. But in spite of its difficulty, communication is vital to anyone who wishes to succeed or make a difference in this world. Our best ideas will be of little use if we can't express them in ways other people can understand.

For a beginning student of rhetoric, the best first step is to consider the **purposes** of writing. Most writers (and speakers, for that matter) have at least one of four basic purposes in mind. The author of a textbook writes **to inform**—to share useful and perhaps interesting knowledge with readers. When the editor of a newspaper prepares his daily editorial, he usually intends **to persuade**—to convince his subscribers they should support the local United Way campaign, approve the building of a new bridge, stop littering, or re-elect their state senator. A minister toiling over her Sunday sermon or weekly essay for the church bulletin is writing **to inspire**—that is, she is urging her congregation to hold fast to their convictions and work hard for what they believe. The writer of science fiction aims **to entertain**—to make his readers feel excited and happy, to make them laugh or cry.

It is important to note that a writer often has more than one purpose. A good sports article might be both informative and entertaining. A science fiction novel about a daring hero might be inspirational as well as entertaining. An inspiring sermon might contain information about daily life in Biblical times, and if that information were especially interesting, the sermon would also be entertaining. Nevertheless, it would still be true that the sports writer's first or **primary** purpose is to inform, the preacher's first purpose is to inspire, and the novelist's first task is to entertain.

This book will focus primarily on informative and persuasive writing, the subjects of Parts One and Two. Part Three will deal with the use of logic in persuasive writing, while Parts Four and Five focus on fallacies, falsehoods, propaganda, and distortions of logic. Our study will conclude with a survey of the creative process.

Name _____ Date _____

Assignment: The Uses of Communication

1. On a typical day, each of us communicates in speech or writing with a number of different people. With which people do you speak regularly? _____

_____

_____

2. Do you write to anyone on a regular basis? (your English teacher? a relative who lives in a distant town? a pen pal? your favorite chat group on the Internet?) _____

_____

_____

3. Suppose you were a teacher. With whom would you be required to communicate in speech? in writing? _____

_____

_____

_____

4. Now suppose you were running for mayor of your city. Why would it be important for you to communicate well? _____

_____

_____

_____

5. If you were a nationally-known athletic star, would it be important for you to communicate? With whom? _____

_____

_____

_____

6. Why is communication an important skill for the owner of a business?

_____

_____

_____

PART ONE: WRITING TO INFORM

1. Information, Please

All of us need information. Our ability to live in the world—to earn a living, to get along with friends and family members, to vote intelligently, to enjoy sports and the arts—depends upon knowledge. We gain some of our most important knowledge by *experience*—the people we meet and the things that happen to us every day. But the world is too wide for us to explore it fully on our own. When experience fails us, we often turn to writers and books to expand our supply of information.

Writers share their information in many ways. Every student is familiar with the textbook, of course; but a curious reader can also find information in newspapers and magazines. Bookstores and libraries are gold mines of information: biographies, reference books, self-help books, books about current events, even books about how to study successfully. Do you have an unusual interest or hobby—kite flying? doorknob collecting? the care and breeding of garter snakes? No matter how eccentric or offbeat your interest may be, chances are that somebody somewhere has written a book or a story in a magazine about it.

Writers also prepare scripts for television and radio newscasts. More and more people are also learning new information today by way of the Internet, and many writers are eager to share their ideas and knowledge by means of the computer.

Do you have any information the world might find useful or enjoyable? Are you a good baby sitter? Have you perfected the art of the slam-dunk? Can you plant a garden or build a perfect campsite? Are you in a position to understand the special problems in your school, neighborhood, town, or city? If so, you should consider the advantages of writing an **informative essay.**

But before you start pouring out facts and ideas in the first words that come to mind, remember that such a method will confuse most readers rather than enlighten them. Instead, you should consider the many methods or **strategies** you can use to organize and present your information clearly, in ways most people can easily understand. In the next few pages, we will examine several of the most popular methods: **narration, description, exemplification, definition, classification,** and **casual reasoning.** With a little practice, you too can add your best efforts to the important task of keeping the world informed.

Name _____ Date _____

ASSIGNMENT: Information, Please!

1. What sort of information would you need in order to become a good athlete? _____

_____

   To become a movie star? _____

_____

   To choose the best candidates in an election for officers of the student council? _____

_____

   To prepare a complete Thanksgiving dinner? _____

_____

   To run for President of the United States? _____

_____

   To travel around the world in a sailboat?_____

_____

   To start your own business? _____

_____

2. What information would be most helpful to you at this time in your life?

_____

_____

_____

3. Where could you go to find this information?

_____

_____

4. What sorts of information have you learned from your own experience?

_____

_____

_____

5. Can you think of anyone who might find your information useful? Who?

_____

_____

4

PART ONE: WRITING TO INFORM

2. Writing a Narrative

To **narrate** means to tell a story. When a writer invents a tale about imaginary people doing imaginary things, we say he is writing **fiction.** Every English-speaking reader is familiar with long works of fiction, called **novels,** such as Mark Twain's *Adventures of Huckleberry Finn.* Fiction also includes **short stories,** like Edgar Allan Poe's "The Pit and the Pendulum" and Washington Irving's "The Legend of Sleepy Hollow." But many writers prefer to tell true stories—accounts of real people and places—which are called **nonfiction.** Because most people love good stories, the **narrative** method is one of the most effective ways possible to present information.

Historians and biographers write nonfiction narratives; so do journalists of all kinds, including sports writers. Even psychologists and other scientists have good stories to tell. Several decades ago, a pair of psychologists were called upon to treat a most unusual patient—a woman named Eve who was convinced that she was really three different people. The psychologists eventually wrote a book telling the story of their successful effort to treat Eve and help her live a normal life. This book, *The Three Faces of Eve,* was so fascinating that it became a best-seller and was made into a successful motion picture.

Every good narrative involves some kind of struggle or **conflict.** This struggle might be highly dramatic—the crew of the *Apollo 13* fighting to return to Earth alive, a doctor's heroic effort to find a cure for a desperately ill patient, the underdog Prairie View Coyotes scrambling to defeat the top-rated Springfield Panthers at basketball. Or the conflict might be more subtle. A travel writer describing a joyful trip to Hawaii would not exactly be dealing in life-or-death adventure. Still, every journey is a conflict—against gravity, as the traveler hauls her baggage out of the car and drags it to the fourth story of the hotel, or against time, as she rushes to reach her destinations. Great or small, the conflict must always be there if the narrative is to capture a reader's interest.

If you want to write a good narrative—or do any kind of informative writing, for that matter—you must learn to write an **introduction** that will immediately capture attention and arouse curiosity. For a narrative, this means that in the opening sentences you should give some hint of the conflict to come, like this:

At last my dream was about to come true! After months of saving dimes and quarters, reading brochures, and making frantic telephone calls to the Springfield airport, I would at last walk along the beaches of Hawaii—if I could somehow pack my suitcase, deliver my dog to the boarding kennel, drive to the airport, and get myself past the check-in counter in only two hours.

After you have written the introduction, you should get quickly into the most interesting part of your narrative. Resist the temptation to linger over unimportant matters. Sometimes a beginning writer will get lost in details. If she is trying to tell the story of a trip to Hawaii, she will list everything she packed in the suitcase (a beach towel, three tubes of tanning oil, a sweater in case of a freakish cold spell), then describe how the dog crawled under the house and had to be lured out with a package of turkey bologna. By the time she finally gets herself to the airport, she has run out of paper. To avoid this pitfall, you might start by making a list of the three or four most important, exciting, or funny events that will be included in your narrative. Such a list can serve as a kind of road map when you write your essay. Remember to save your most important or exciting material for the end.

Name _____ Date _____

ASSIGNMENT: Thinking About Narratives

1. Look through the Sunday edition of a major newspaper. How many narratives can you find? List some of them. _____

_____

_____

2. Have you ever had any personal experiences that would make interesting narratives—perhaps an exciting victory in sports, a wonderful or ghastly vacation, a harrowing accident, a troublesome pet, a concert or recital where everything went wrong? List a few such experiences. _____

_____

_____

3. Choose an item from your list, think of an interesting title, and write an opening paragraph for a narrative essay. Remember that your introduction must capture attention or arouse curiosity. _____

_____

_____

_____

_____

_____

4. List three or four important episodes that need to be included in your narrative.

    A. _____
    B. _____
    C. _____
    D. _____

5. Complete the essay on your own paper. Remember to put your title at the top of the page.

PART ONE: WRITING TO INFORM

3. Writing a Description

"One picture is worth a thousand words," people say. But a writer can use words to create a picture in a reader's mind—a picture that could put the best photograph to shame—because a good **description** appeals not only to the eyes, but also to the ears, the nose, the sense of touch, and the taste buds.

Descriptive writing has many uses. Suppose, for example, that your school needs a new gymnasium because the old one is falling down—literally. The roof leaks, the floor boards are rotten, water is everywhere—except in the showers, where the faucets can barely manage to drip. You have decided to write a letter to the local newspaper, urging the citizens to vote for a tax increase to build a new gym. How better to make your case than by describing the old gymnasium in all its leaky, rotten, mildewed glory? If you want your description to be especially memorable, be sure to **appeal to all of the senses.** Your readers should not only be able to see the damage, but also to hear the plunk of raindrops on the floor, smell the growing fungi, and feel the discouraging slop of dirty water against their new running shoes.

Are you tired of writing the same old boring history papers about names, places, and dates? If so, you might try a descriptive paper for your next history assignment. If your project is an essay on Dolley Madison, you could describe her at a grand occasion in the White House drawing room—Dolley Madison, one of the most famous hostesses in history, looking every inch a queen in her velvet gown, long train, pearl necklace and earrings, and fashionable plumed turban from Paris. Let us see her elegant guests: women in diamonds and satin evening dresses; men in coats of blue, green, and scarlet; an ambassador wearing a fancy dress sword and a uniform trimmed in gold lace—and Dolley moving gracefully around the room, remembering everyone's name, putting all of her guests at ease, gently reassuring a shy, young man who has just dropped and broken a saucer…

But before you get completely carried away, remember that descriptive writing has several dangers. One such danger is the temptation to fill the page with adjectives instead of relying on forceful nouns and lively verbs. Long strings of adjectives—especially the ten-dollar words like *sumptuous, resplendent, luminescent,* and *scintillating*—will do your paper no good. Another bad habit of descriptive writers is a tendency to ramble. Back in the nineteenth century, when Charles Dickens was alive, most people loved long descriptions and would have been disappointed if a book were too short for much description. Tastes have changed, however, and most modern readers like their prose to be brief and vivid. You can satisfy such readers if, instead of trying to describe everything, you focus only on the most interesting, most striking details.

Name _____ Date _____

ASSIGNMENT: Writing a Description

1. Write the name or location of a favorite place. _____
_____

2. Imagine you are standing or sitting in this place. What things do you see? _____
_____
_____

3. Can you hear anything? What? _____
_____
_____

4. Can you smell anything? _____
_____
_____

5. What is the temperature like—mild, hot, or cold? Is it humid or dry? _____
_____
_____

6. Is any food available? If so, what? How does it taste? _____
_____
_____

7. Do you feel any unusual sensations? Does your heart beat fast, or do you shiver with excitement? Is a gentle breeze blowing? Do you feel completely relaxed and calm? Is water lapping against your toes?
_____
_____
_____

8. Now read your list and circle the details that would be most interesting to read about in a description. Write your description on your own paper, and remember to give your paper a title.

　　　OR, if you prefer, make a separate list about a place that you hate or one that frightens you, and describe that place instead.

PART ONE: WRITING TO INFORM

4. Writing With Examples

One of the best ways to make a point is to give **examples.** Suppose you were to state that people rarely follow their own best advice. Will your friends nod their heads in agreement? Probably not, unless you go on to illustrate. Tell them about Joe, for example, who preaches about the importance of organization but whose locker is so messy that whenever he opens the door, an avalanche of books and papers tumbles to the floor. And Sally, who cries "Everyone stay calm!" as she becomes hysterical over the smallest problems. Then there's Mr. Carter, a teacher who harangues his students about the importance of planning ahead but who can never finish calculating his grades in time to meet the deadline. Mr. Carter's wife extols thrift and saving even as she runs up huge bills on her ten credit cards. And don't forget Miss Hefflefinger—who, between sermons about the importance of kindness and consideration, is constantly throwing temper tantrums and insulting everyone in sight.

Every writer should learn to use examples, because they are an important form of **evidence** (a subject we will examine in detail, starting in Chapter 11). But how many examples are enough to make a point? A writer can choose among several methods. He might give a number of brief examples (as I have just done in the preceding paragraph), but he will probably make things more interesting, both for himself and his readers, if he concentrates on three or four of the best examples, devoting several sentences or paragraphs to each one. He might even find it useful to devote an entire essay to one remarkable example—to write at length about Miss Hefflefinger, perhaps, and her many peculiarities. Although such an essay might well be amusing or thought-provoking, a writer should keep in mind that **one example proves nothing.** When somebody jumps to a conclusion without considering enough evidence, he is guilty of **hasty generalization,** a matter we will consider further in our section on logic.

If you want to make good use of examples, you might consider a useful type of essay known as the **three-point enumeration.** Such a paper is easy to organize and write. Start with an introductory paragraph that will catch the reader's attention and make him want to read further: ask a question, describe a conflict or problem, raise an issue, make a surprising statement, such as "Advice!—everyone gives it, but almost nobody practices what he or she preaches." Follow the introduction with three more paragraphs, each one devoted to a different example: Joe and his locker, Mrs. Carter and her ten credit cards, Miss Hefflefinger and her terrible temper. Remember to save your best example for the fourth paragraph. Conclude with a short paragraph that states your main idea: We would all be better and happier people if we would sometimes listen to our own words of wisdom.

Name _____ Date _____

ASSIGNMENT: Using Examples

Select one of the following statements: A penny saved is a penny earned; a stitch in time saves nine; practice makes perfect; a fool and his money are soon parted; never put off until tomorrow what you can do today; if at first you don't succeed, try, try again; treat others as you would have them treat you; look before you leap; practice what you preach; be prepared.

1. Think of and list three good examples that illustrate the statement you selected:

   A. _____

   _____

   _____

   _____

   B. _____

   _____

   _____

   _____

   C. _____

   _____

   _____

   _____

2. Write a good title for your essay: _____

3. List some interesting ways to begin and end your paper: _____

_____

_____

_____

_____

4. Write the essay on your own paper. Include five paragraphs, and remember to put your title at the top of the page.

PART ONE: WRITING TO INFORM

5. Definition

Suppose the school board of Springfield appoints a committee to improve education at Madison Junior High School. The committee consists of four of Madison's best teachers: Mr. Jones, Mrs. Smith, Miss Brown, and Coach Robinson. At their first meeting, the committee members get along beautifully: all four of them agree that "education" can and should be improved at Madison School, and they are enthusiastic about their mission and about the committee. But by the time the second meeting is over, the four teachers have already begun fighting among themselves. Each has a different idea: Mr. Jones wants to add business courses to help students find jobs; Mrs. Smith wants to hire more history teachers so the students will learn to be informed voters; Miss Brown wants to start a literary magazine to develop the students' creativity; and Coach Robinson wants a soccer team to build healthy bodies. As the weeks go by, the teachers discover the four of them can never agree on anything, and in the spring the committee breaks up without having accomplished a single improvement at Madison School.

If the teachers had been wiser, they might have devoted their first meeting to a discussion about the word *education.* Can this term be defined? What should a student actually get out of his education—training for a good-paying job? a wholesome personality? the ability to be a responsible citizen? good health and a strong body? It is difficult, often impossible, for people to have intelligent discussions unless they can agree on the definitions of important words.

Some words are easy to define. If a math student asks his teacher to define the word *compass,* she can do so quite easily by showing a compass to her students and then demonstrating how it is used to draw a perfect circle. If you ask your mother to define the word *tetrazzini,* she can make a tetrazzini casserole and then give you a taste of it. But words such as *education, freedom, democracy, creativity, goodness, evil,* and *religion* are more difficult to explain. No teacher can give a five-minute classroom definition of *goodness,* and we have no book of recipes for *freedom, democracy, religion,* and *education.* The people of the world will probably never agree on the exact meanings of these words. However, a good writer can sometimes help to clear the confusion by composing an essay of **definition.**

When you are writing a definition, you have your choice of a number of methods. Sometimes you can define a word by **explaining what it does or how it works.** In an essay on democracy, for example, you might describe how the citizens work together to elect their leaders—and, perhaps more important, how they can get rid of a leader who proves untrustworthy or work to repeal a bad law. In an essay entitled "What Is an Athlete?", you might picture what a good athlete does every day—rises at dawn, eats a nutritious breakfast, arrives early at the gym for her morning workout, and so forth. Or, to define a word like *education,* you might make use of **contrast** and describe the very different lives of Jessica, who went to excellent schools, and John, whose education was slipshod and haphazard. Sometimes you can define a word by **explaining what it is not.** In an essay on scientists, for example, you might point out that most scientists are nothing like the "mad" variety pictured in movies and on television—the long-haired, wild-eyed, cackling maniacs who spend long, solitary hours inventing time machines and doomsday devices. Finally, you might define a word like *courage* by giving several **examples** of men and women whom you consider to be especially brave. Writing a good definition can be a difficult task, but—as teachers Jones, Smith, Brown, and Robinson would understand—it is worth the effort.

Name _____ Date _____

ASSIGNMENT: The Essay of Definition

Choose one of the following words: *education, freedom, courage, sportsmanship, family, parent, fairness, athlete, teacher, student, musician, volunteer, citizenship, Boy Scout, Girl Scout, farmer, baby-sitter.*

1. Explain why it is a good idea for people to understand the meaning of this word.

_____

_____

_____

2. What would be the best method of defining this word? _____

_____

_____

3. List three or four main points you would like to make in your essay. _____

_____

_____

_____

_____

4. Write your essay on your own paper. Aim for three to five paragraphs. Don't forget to give your essay a title.

PART ONE: WRITING TO INFORM

6. Classification

We humans love to place things into categories. Scientists divide the animals into different species. High schools and colleges classify their students as freshmen, sophomores, juniors, and seniors; and they categorize their courses as sciences, fine arts, language studies, and so on. Cooks divide their menus into appetizers, main courses, salads, and desserts. Grocers label the aisles of supermarkets. Automakers classify their vehicles as sedans, station wagons, sports cars, vans, and pickup trucks. Politicians describe the voters as liberals, conservatives, moderates, and radicals. **Classification** is our way of creating order in an often-confusing world.

Life would be difficult without classifications. Imagine trying to get through school without knowing whether you were in the first, eighth, or twelfth grade. Or suppose that instead of studying English, math, and history, all of your academic subjects were scrambled together without any kind of order. And wouldn't it be frustrating to shop in a bookstore where all the books were thrown together helter skelter, with no attempt to separate them into categories of nonfiction, mysteries, science fiction, westerns, romances, self-help, and juveniles?

Classification can sometimes shed light on a problem. Suppose the faculty and staff of Madison School decided to improve their sports program so more students will participate and enjoy the benefits of regular exercise. Most of the teachers, when they hear the word "sports," will immediately think of football, basketball, baseball, soccer—the big "team" sports that are broadcast around the nation. But if the faculty and administration really want to attract more students to the sports program, they ought to remember that "sports" also includes such individual activities as equestrian events, archery, diving, and gymnastics, as well as games like tennis and golf. If an athletics program is to serve all of the students, it must include many categories of sports, not just one. A girl who stumbles all over the basketball court might turn out to be the picture of grace on horseback, and a boy who is too small for football could be the state champion at archery.

Classifications are useful, but one word of warning: classify sports and groceries if you will, but don't be too quick to put labels on people. Don't jump to the conclusion, for example, that Joe is a "lazy slob" because his books and papers are such a mess. It may be true that his locker looks like a small nuclear explosion, but at least he can find what he

needs when he needs it; and maybe the reason why he never cleans his locker is that he spends all his spare time keeping his car in perfect order or looking after his little brother. Also beware of statements like this: "There are three kinds of people in this school: jocks, snobs, and nerds." Human life is rarely simple enough to divide like the pieces of a pie.

Name _____ Date _____

ASSIGNMENT: Thinking about Classifications

1. What types of sports are available to the students in your school or city? What kinds of clubs and other activities? _____

_____

_____

2. What types of books do you enjoy most? What types of movies? _____

_____

_____

3. Spend some time at a fast-food restaurant. What different types of people do you see?

_____

_____

4. People attend sporting events for different reasons. What are some of these reasons?

_____

_____

5. What different types of music do you hear frequently? _____

_____

6. What different types of assignments do you receive at your school? _____

_____

7. If you were to buy a purebred dog, what breeds would you consider? Why?

_____

_____

8. What does the word *freedom* mean to you? Are there different ways of being free? What are they? _____

_____

_____

9. On your own paper, write an essay based upon one of these classifications.

PART ONE: WRITING TO INFORM

7. Causes and Effects

Some people are great believers in the value of anger. When they see problems, their approach is to throw fits of outrage, to write letters that bristle with fury, to shout in protest at meetings, and to raise a fuss in general. What better way, they ask, to draw attention to the problems of the world? In fact, is there any other way?

These people have a point: history teaches us that anger indeed has its uses. However, we would do well to remember that even a goat or a mule can get angry, but only a human being can use his brain. Often the first step in solving a problem is *to determine what caused the problem in the first place.* All the anger in the world will not cure a sick man; a doctor must learn the cause of the illness and then prescribe suitable medicine.

All of us are familiar with **cause-and-effect reasoning** in our daily lives. Your history teacher returns your test paper with a grade of "C-minus," and you are bewildered: you were expecting an "A." True, you can be grateful your low grade was not an "F," but you need to keep a high average in order to be eligible for the debate team, and a "C-minus" will not be good enough at the end of the term. Your first response may be to blame the history teacher for being unfair, but after taking some time to calm down, you try to determine the most likely *cause* of your low grade. Did you study the wrong material? Did you stay up too late the night before the test? Should you start taking notes during class? Would it help to study early in the morning instead of late at night? If you can find the cause of your poor performance in history, you can begin working on improvement.

Here is another example: Everyone is shocked when the Springfield High School Panthers lose resoundingly in a basketball game with the Prairie View Coyotes, a team with little experience and a dismal record. The next day, some of the more hot-tempered citizens of Springfield are already calling for the coach's resignation—he's obviously incompetent if his team can't beat those pathetic little Coyotes. Fortunately, most people in Springfield realize the coach needs time to ponder the cause of the Panthers' humiliating defeat. Are the Panthers starting to get out of condition? Were they overconfident on the night of the game? Had several of them caught the flu virus that was going around? Had they been celebrating their string of victories with too many late-night parties? Or was experience finally starting to pay off for the Coyotes?

Meanwhile, back in Prairie View, the Coyotes' coach is whooping for joy. But after he has finished celebrating, he too must start thinking about causes and effects. Not even he had expected the stunning upset victory; obviously he and his players have done *something* right—but what? He must find out so he can coach his team to more such thrilling victories!

It is difficult to study causes and effects, because most situations have more than one cause, and often the cause of a problem is less obvious than it seems (more about this in Chapter 17). But, for a writer who enjoys a challenge, the cause-and-effect essay can be a worthwhile project.

Name _____ Date _____

ASSIGNMENT: Causes and Effects

A. Write the name of a well-known person whom you particularly admire.

_____

1. What caused this person's rise to fame? In other words, what are the reasons why you (and many other people) admire him or her? Try to think of three or four reasons.

_____

_____

_____

_____

_____

2. On your own paper, develop this list into an essay.

B. Do you have a hobby, special interest, favorite activity, or favorite subject in school?

1. Describe it briefly. _____

_____

_____

2. What caused you to become interested in this activity? _____

_____

_____

3. What is the effect of this activity on your life? Does it help you relax or give you a chance to make new friends? Does it help you earn or save money? Will it help you get a job some day? _____

_____

_____

_____

_____

4. On your own paper, write an essay about your favorite activity.

PART TWO: WRITING TO PERSUADE

8. The Importance of Persuasion

Strictly speaking, an **informative** writer deals with facts and explanations. He is not supposed to preach, give advice, or otherwise express opinions of his own. Writers of textbooks and reference books deal with information; so do most reporters for newspapers and magazines.

Whenever a conflict arises, informative writers rush to the scene. Imagine, for example, that the principal of Prairie View High School wants to build a new parking lot next to the gymnasium. She insists that more and better parking is needed so elderly citizens and handicapped people can attend basketball games without being forced to park their cars on a faraway side street and then walk for half a mile along darkened and crumbling sidewalks. But in order to build the new parking spaces, somebody will have to cut down a number of trees on the vacant lot next to the gymnasium, and the members of the Prairie View Garden Club are indignantly opposed to the scheme. In their opinion, Prairie View would be better served if the vacant lot were turned into a pleasant park with fountains and benches—an appropriate setting for all those lovely trees. What does Prairie View need with one more ugly parking lot? Let the sports fans walk! They, of all people, should know exercise is healthy!

The typical newspaper reporter will probably choose to prepare an *informative* article about this conflict. He will interview people on both sides of the issue—the school principal, an elderly sports fan, the leaders of the Garden Club, members of the Hug-a-Tree Society. In his article, he will include such *facts* as the location of the gym, the distance from the gym to the nearest good parking lot, the condition of the sidewalks and street lights near the gym, the number of games each year, the number of people who regularly attend those games, and the number of trees that would have to be cut in order to build the new parking spaces. When his article appears in the paper, anyone who reads it will have a good idea of what the dispute is about. What the reporter will *not* do is take sides. His job is to inform, not to argue.

But while the reporter is busy writing his article, the editor of the newspaper may very well be preparing an editorial urging the citizens to support the principal and her plans for the parking lot. And when the newspaper is published, the editor's column will appear side by side with letters from the Garden Club and the Hug-a-Tree Society, urging the people of Prairie View to protest by refusing to attend any more basketball games until plans for the new parking lot are scrapped. A reputable newspaper has room for both informative writing and **persuasive** writing—articles and essays urging readers to make up their minds, to change their minds, or to take stands on important issues.

The art of **persuasion** is important in every aspect of our lives. After all, we live in a country where people vote for their leaders; hence anyone who wants to be a leader must persuade people to give him their votes and their loyalty. And anyone who has a new idea must persuade the people around him that his idea is worth considering—always a difficult task, because people tend to get comfortable with old ways, and they are often afraid of change. Your teachers must somehow convince you their lessons really do matter, and that it is important to study instead of just watch television, go fishing, or take a nap. Preachers must convince the members of their congregations to get themselves out of bed on Sundays, put on good clothes, and go to church. And anybody who has a gadget to sell must persuade his customers to part with their hard-earned money in exchange for his gizmo.

English teachers often use the word *argument* in place of the word *persuasion.* It is important to understand that in the study of writing, the word *argument* means something quite different from its usual sense of a *quarrel,* in which people get angry and raise their voices. As we shall see in the following pages, you are unlikely to change anyone's mind by shouting insults and waving your fist in the air. Instead, persuasion is an art that must be learned and practiced with care.

Name _____ Date _____

ASSIGNMENT: The Uses of Persuasion

1. Study a recent issue of your local newspaper. What kinds of informative articles (those that deal strictly with facts) can you find? List a few of them. _____

_____

_____

_____

2. On what pages of the newspaper do you find opinions? _____

_____

3. Some people write not to inform or persuade, but to entertain. Can you find any material in the newspaper that is pure entertainment? _____

_____

4. Can you find an article or essay that offers a combination of information, entertainment, and persuasion? _____

_____

5. If your newspaper has a "Letters" column, read a few of the letters over the course of several days. How many of these letters are argumentative? Do any of them persuade you of anything? Why or why not? _____

_____

_____

_____

_____

PART TWO: WRITING TO PERSUADE

9. Know Your Readers

You are beginning your first year as a starter on the Prairie View Fighting Coyotes' basketball team. Your grandfather would like to come to the gymnasium and watch you play, but he suffers from arthritis and is unable to walk long distances to get to the game. Your Aunt Minerva would also like to attend the games, but she is afraid to walk alone in the dark. Although you seldom admit it, you are a little bit nervous about your new role on the starting lineup, and you want your family to be in the bleachers cheering when you run onto the court. You support the new parking lot one hundred percent, and you're going to write to the local newspaper and let everyone know. But how can you convince the people of Prairie View that you are right?

Naturally, your first impulse may be to scribble something like "It isn't *fair* that my own grandfather can't watch me play basketball!" But before you grab your pen and paper, take a deep breath and think about the people who might read your letter in the newspaper. What are they likely to be thinking? A few of them are probably sports fanatics who attend every event that features a ball. A few others, such as the members of the Hug-a-Tree Society, never saw a plant they didn't adore; they even love poison ivy and Venus' fly traps. Then there is a somewhat larger group of people who enjoy trees and like to stroll in a well-kept park. But most citizens of Prairie View probably have no strong opinion at all. Many of them have never before thought about the issue of parks versus parking lots. To which people will you direct your argument?

Not to the sports fans—they are already on your side! Why waste time trying to convince them of something they already believe? And you don't have to worry about the Hug-a-Tree Society; you could never bring them to your point of view, even if you had the combined skill of Shakespeare, Martin Luther King, and Aladdin's genie. Instead, you must *concentrate on the readers who are open-minded or undecided.* These are the ones who may read your letter with interest and give thoughtful consideration to what you have to say.

And when you write your letter, focus *on the issues.* An **issue** is a matter about which reasonable people can disagree. A common mistake is to waste time and paper by straying from the subject. You may be tempted, for example, to devote half of your letter to the importance of a healthy body, but most sensible people are already believers in good health (or at least, we rarely hear anyone claim that a weak and sickly body is better than a strong and healthy body). Indeed, the merits of basketball and the benefits of physical fitness are beside the point. If you want to be persuasive, you must focus on the specific issue at hand: whether to build a park or a parking lot on the vacant lot next to the Prairie View Gymnasium.

You might also consider the possibility of a **compromise**—a solution that will have some appeal for people on both sides. For example, a good landscape artist could probably design a parking lot with a small park in the center and trees around all four sides. Such a plan would allow plenty of new parking space, while saving at least some of the trees. And the new parking lot would have the added advantage of being shady and cool in July and August—a big attraction for people who might enroll in the school's summer fitness program.

19

As you prepare your letter, keep in mind the difference between persuasive writing and **inspirational** writing. The two must not be confused. A persuasive writer attempts to change his readers' minds; an inspirational writer urges readers to hold fast to *ideas they already believe.* For example, in her annual spring address to the Garden Club, the president will probably remind her audience about the importance of planting trees, weeding gardens, spreading the flower beds with plant food—in a word, making the world a more beautiful place. Such a speech might seem like a waste of time—after all, the members are already enthusiastic gardeners; otherwise they would never have joined the club in the first place. True enough, but even the most enthusiastic gardeners can grow tired or out of sorts; they need an occasional jolt of energy, a reminder that their work is really important.

Notice that the president of the Garden Club has a relatively easy task. She need not win her audience over; they are already on her side. If she can come up with some fine-sounding phrases about the loveliness of flowers and the importance of making Prairie View beautiful, her members will be ready to rush out the door and grab their shovels. But the persuasive writer or speaker has no such comfort. His audience is undecided, wary, skeptical, maybe even hostile. He has his work cut out for him. He must make good use of facts and evidence; he must also try to understand his opponents.

Name _____ Date _____

ASSIGNMENT: Understanding the Reader

1. If you were a citizen of Prairie View, what arguments would convince you to support the construction of a new parking lot near the gymnasium? _____

_____

_____

_____

_____

2. What sort of argument might convince you that a park, not a parking lot, is a better idea?

_____

_____

_____

_____

_____

PART TWO: WRITING TO PERSUADE

10. Your Worthy Opponent

Rich Mr. Beezley dies, and in his will he leaves a large sum of money to your school. (Well, you can dream.) As members of the student council, you and several of your friends have the delightful task of deciding how to spend the money. Because your dream is to go to law school and become the next Perry Mason, you believe Mr. Beezley's money can best be used to improve the library—to purchase new books, videos, computer programs, and other materials that will help you prepare for your chosen career. Your classmate, Brad, is also on the council, and you are sure of his support; after all, he is the most conscientious student in school, and he has a straight-A record. Furthermore, he is an enthusiastic student; he seems to enjoy every class he takes. His goal is to become a newspaper reporter and someday an editor.

Much to your surprise, however, you discover that Brad is opposed to your plan. He wants to spend the money on new uniforms for the marching band. You are bewildered by Brad's attitude. True, the old uniforms have been around for several years and have seen a lot of marching; but they look to you as if they have plenty of wear left. Brad is being selfish, you think, because he is the drum major and he wants to strut around the football stadium in a flashy new uniform. Eventually the principal schedules a debate before the student body, and you are chosen to present the case for a better library. Brad will argue the case for band uniforms. What will you say to your fellow students to convince them that you are right and Brad is wrong?

You may be angry at Brad for opposing your plan, but remember it is wise to **be fair to your opponent.** What if you were to vent your anger and claim that Brad is opposed to improving the library because he is stupid, lazy, and irresponsible, the sort of goof-off who would rather loll in front of the television set than read a book or learn a new computer program? If you make such a speech, you will almost certainly lose the respect of your audience, because everyone, including you, will know your charges are untrue. And, if you are smart, you will not proclaim music is a foolish waste of time and money. After all, there will be a lot of musicians in the audience—not just the band members, but also the choir members, the people who take piano and organ lessons, and the cast of the school's production of *The Sound of Music.* You can't afford to offend so many people; you may need their votes.

Instead, you might prepare for the debate by **looking at the situation from your opponent's point of view.** You know Brad is intelligent and well-organized, and you can assume he will plan his speech with care. When you are preparing for the debate, make a list of the reasons why Brad might choose new uniforms over books and computer programs. Then try to think of an answer or counter-argument for each point he might raise. And when you prepare your own side of the debate, you will need to do more than talk about your dream of going to law school, because if you sound selfish, you will lose support. Instead, think of reasons why a good library would benefit the entire school—students, teachers, parents, everyone.

21

Name _____ Date _____

ASSIGNMENT: Your Opponent's Point of View

1. Brad is an enthusiastic student. Why does he support the marching band instead of the library? List as many reasons as you can think of.

_____

_____

_____

_____

2. On your own paper, write a speech supporting the purchase of library materials instead of band uniforms. Or, if you prefer, take Brad's side of the issue and argue in favor of the uniforms. Whichever side you take, remember to **be fair to your opponent.**

3. Ms. Yapp and Mr. Zilch are running for mayor of your city. Ms. Yapp wants to raise taxes in order to mend the many potholes in the city streets. Mr. Zilch wants to lower taxes so the citizens will have more money to spend at the local stores and restaurants. When the two candidates meet each other in debate, what will be Ms. Yapp's main points? List as many as you can think of.

_____

_____

_____

_____

_____

4. What will be Mr. Zilch's main arguments? _____

_____

_____

_____

_____

5. On your own paper, write a letter to the editor of your local paper, supporting either Ms. Yapp or Mr. Zilch for mayor.

PART TWO: WRITING TO PERSUADE

11. What Is Evidence?

Every lover of murder mysteries is familiar with **evidence.** The typical mystery story or novel begins with a crime, usually a puzzling murder: Dr. Blatt, president of the school board, is found shot to death in his office, cruelly murdered with his own cherished antique pistol—or did he commit suicide? The police aren't certain. Dr. Blatt was kindhearted in his own gruff way, but in spite of his good intentions, he had made a number of enemies over the years. One week before his death, he had quarreled loudly with Mr. Bravo, the director of the high school's marching band, and the entire trumpet section had heard Mr. Bravo shout, "I've had all I can stand, and I'm not going to put up with you any longer!" About the same time, a rumor had spread that Dr. Blatt was trying to get Ms. Prissy fired from her job as assistant school librarian in charge of maps. (Ms. Prissy had recently joined the Flat Earth Society and was demanding that all world globes be destroyed or removed from classrooms and libraries.) Dr. Blatt's daughter, Petunia, had an excellent motive for murder: she is the heir to her father's money. And lately several of Dr. Blatt's neighbors had noticed a strange-looking man in green overalls who kept turning up at Dr. Blatt's back door just at sunset. Which of these suspects committed the foul murder—if indeed it was murder? Nobody knows of a reason why Dr. Blatt might kill himself, but Dr. Blatt rarely confided in anyone.

Enter the detective—Sherlock Holmes, Hercule Poirot, Jessica Fletcher, Miss Marple, or Lieutenant Columbo. The detective must solve the crime before an innocent man or woman is convicted and sent to jail.

Every mystery fan knows what must happen next: The detective studies the **evidence.** He looks for clues. He notices a cup and saucer on Dr. Blatt's desk; it appears Dr. Blatt served tea to a visitor on the day of his death. The handle of the teacup is pointing to the left-hand side of the desk; and later, when the detective asks Ms. Prissy to hand him some papers, he notices she is left-handed. He talks to all of the suspects, their friends, and their families, and he discovers that when Ms. Prissy was sixteen years old, she was president of her high school's Target-Shooting Club. The man in the green overalls turns out to be an exterminator who works the night shift. If an exterminator wanted to kill somebody, wouldn't he use poison instead of a gun? Mr. Bravo appears to have an ironclad alibi: he was conducting a band rehearsal at the time of the murder, and every band member saw him on the podium. Petunia claims to have been at home alone, and when the detective questions her neighbors, they remember that her car had stood in the driveway during the entire day of the murder. Whom does the detective suspect?

Whatever he decides, his conclusion must be *based on evidence, not on his feelings.* He will be laughed out of court if he tells a jury, "Obviously the exterminator is guilty, because I hate the color green, and I've never trusted people who wear overalls!" or "You should convict Ms. Prissy because she has eyes like a snake's!" Of course, intuition and emotions may guide the detective as he conducts his investigation. If Ms. Prissy's snakelike eyes make his blood run cold, he might find it prudent to take a close look at her youthful career as a target-shooter. But, he may not make a public accusation of Ms. Prissy until and unless he has enough evidence to prove his claim. If he is too quick to accuse, the result will be chaos, not justice.

The detective is allowed to have feelings, of course; otherwise he would hardly be a human being. Emotions make it possible for him to enjoy art and music, to build friendships, and to love his family. (Sherlock Holmes enjoyed listening to violin music, Jessica Fletcher won many friends, and Lieutenant Columbo apparently loved his wife very much.) Furthermore, it is the detective's emotion—his passion for justice and truth—that gives him the energy to keep plugging away at his investigation day after day, even when good sense might tell him to give up and make a reservation at the golf course. But the detective can prove nothing with feelings. Only evidence can send the murderer to prison.

Anyone who wants to be persuasive must learn to **build a case with evidence.** If you really want to convince your friends that your school needs library materials more urgently than it needs band uniforms, then you have to do more than just say so. You'll also have to offer more than a solemn talk about how books are the most noble creations of the human race and computers are the key to the future. You'll have to do some detective work and find some hard evidence. How many books does the State Department of Education recommend for a good school library, and how many books does your library actually own? How many of these books are more than twenty years old? How old are the programs in the computer lab? Does the librarian complain about outdated materials and a small budget? Do your friends complain about long waiting lists to get the books they need for school assignments? Do they give up in disgust and make trips downtown to the city library? It is up to you to provide the answers to these questions. If the evidence shows the library is inadequate for the school's needs, then you will probably win your case.

Name _____ Date _____

ASSIGNMENT: Questions for Thought

1. If your television set is hooked to cable or to a satellite, watch an episode of *Murder, She Wrote* or *Columbo.* How do these televised mysteries compare to Doyle's stories about Sherlock Holmes?

_____

_____

_____

2. Many fictional detectives are rather strange people. For example, Nero Wolfe is incredibly fat, he seldom leaves his house, and the passions of his life are eating gourmet food and raising orchids. Lieutenant Columbo wears a rumpled raincoat and drives a broken-down car, and he always acts as if he were feebleminded. Can you think of any reasons why authors portray detectives in this way?

_____

_____

_____

PART TWO: WRITING TO PERSUADE

12. True Facts, False Facts, and Factoids

"The true facts are that the city of Springfield has the freshest air, the purest water, and the most beautiful parks in all of America!" Thus speaks the mayor of Springfield as he opens the town's annual Civic Pride Festival. The mayor's love for his city is touching, but two questions come to mind: first, isn't he repeating himself when he uses the phrase "true facts"? Does His Honor really believe in such things as false facts? And second, how could he possibly know whether Springfield has the freshest air, the cleanest water, and the most beautiful parks in all fifty states? Has he made a grand tour of every town in America, sipping at water fountains, inhaling deeply, and inspecting each park along the way? What exactly does he mean when he talks about facts?

In order for a piece of information to be a **fact,** it must be something that can be and has been proven beyond any sensible doubt. We say for a *fact* that the earth is round, and we can offer a great deal of **evidence** as proof. For one thing, we have seen the earth's shadow on the face of the moon—a distinctly round shadow. Our ships have sailed around the earth, our airplanes have flown around it, and astronauts and satellites have taken the earth's picture from outer space. Of course, there are a few people, like Ms. Prissy of the Flat Earth Society, who insist the photographs and the entire Apollo space program were faked, but no one takes these arguments seriously. For all but a few people, the great round earth is a fact.

Unfortunately, many people use the word *fact* when they are really talking about *opinion*—as the mayor of Springfield does when he praises his city's parks as the most beautiful in the nation. Of course, we should forgive the mayor for his exaggerations; after all, mayors are supposed to say patriotic things at festivals. But a persuasive writer should always be careful not to confuse fact with opinion. How can we tell the difference? Remember that facts can be proven; opinions often cannot. For example, a historian can confidently talk about the facts of Thomas Jefferson's life—that he lived in a house called Monticello, that he was an ingenious inventor, and that he designed many of the buildings at the University of Virginia. Anyone who doubts these facts can check for himself in the reference books; if he doesn't believe what he reads in the books, he can travel to Virginia and visit Monticello, where some of Jefferson's inventions are on display, and he will see the evidence with his own eyes.

But a good historian will be wary of stating that Jefferson was the greatest president or the wisest scholar in the history of America. Admirers of Washington, Lincoln, and the Roosevelts might disagree, and how can a historian offer convincing proof of greatness and wisdom? He certainly can't measure such qualities with a tape measure or dissolve them in liquid for study under a microscope. The historian has every right to express an opinion about Jefferson's greatness, but he has no right to call his opinion a fact.

Writers and historians should also beware of **factoids.** The word *factoid* was invented by artist Norman Mailer. What is a factoid? Well, just as a *humanoid* or *android* robot is a machine that looks like a man or woman, a factoid is a piece of misinformation that looks like a fact. Factoids are things that "everyone knows"—but that aren't true. Here's how a factoid comes to life: at two o'clock in the morning, a sleepy reporter is struggling to write a story about fads and fashions among politicians. His deadline is at eight o'clock, and he doesn't have as much information as he needs. He thinks he remembers the vice president once received a pair of purple-and-orange socks for Christmas. So he includes a paragraph about how the vice president likes to wear purple socks with orange polka dots—a harmless exaggeration, he thinks, and it certainly makes his story more interesting. But when his story is published, a number of other reporters read about the purple socks, raise their eyebrows, and include the ugly socks in stories of their own. Soon every well-read American "knows" about the vice president's ghastly socks, and some people are beginning to wonder whether the vice president ought to be dropped from the ticket at election time. What if he accidentally becomes president and starts greeting kings and ambassadors while wearing those hideous polka-dotted socks? The ambassadors would be insulted; kings might declare war! The truth is, however, that the vice president owns no polka-dotted socks of any color; the story of the socks is a factoid.

Name _____ Date _____

ASSIGNMENT: Facts and Evidence

Senator Foghorn is running for re-election. The following is a passage from one of his campaign speeches:

My fellow citizens, when you go to the polls on election day, let the facts speak for themselves. My opponent is the biggest liar who has ever run for office in this state. Why, just look at his long, beak-like nose and sunken eyes! I wouldn't trust anyone who has such an evil-looking face. No, my dear friends, you should have a senator who loves this state the way I do. Do you love this state's beautiful scenery and proud history? Then vote for me, Joseph Q. Foghorn. I will speak bravely about the issues that are important to all of you. My opponent is a lazy, cheating, crooked scoundrel who keeps his hat on in church and spills gravy all over his shirt. Don't you deserve better?

1. What problems can you find in this speech? _____

_____

_____

_____

2. Would you be inclined to vote for Senator Foghorn? Why or why not? _____

_____

_____

_____

PART TWO: WRITING TO PERSUADE

13. Mr. Occam and His Wonderful Razor

William of Occam (also spelled Ockham) was an English scholar and philosopher who lived during the time known as the medieval period or the Middle Ages. Today, if we were to accuse somebody of being "medieval" in his ideas, we would probably mean he was old-fashioned, out of touch with reality, and possibly stupid or cruel. But although William of Occam was a medieval man, his head was so filled with new ideas that he has been called the first modern philosopher. In fact, one of his theories turned out to be so useful that it has become known as **Occam's Razor**, an important principle of modern science.

What exactly is Occam's Razor? It amounts to a belief in simplicity. According to Occam, when one is examining evidence, **it is a mistake to accept a complicated explanation when a simple one will do just as well.**

Here is an illustration: Mr. Jones goes home one afternoon and discovers his dog is missing from the back yard, which is enclosed on all sides by a fence. Mr. Jones takes a look around and notices the gate is firmly closed and latched from the inside. Nobody was at home to let the dog out, and nobody could have opened the gate from the outside. What happened to the dog?

Mr. Jones can assume the dog escaped by jumping over the fence. Or, he can assume a flying saucer swooped out of the sky and touched down in the back yard, and a team of alien scientists (possibly in league with the FBI and the CIA) snatched the poor dog and whisked it away to become the subject of bizarre intergalactic experiments at a secret laboratory somewhere in the deserts of Utah.

Notice that either theory will explain the disappearance of Mr. Jones's dog. But Mr. Jones knows that dogs sometimes jump over fences, and he has no evidence of flying saucers or alien scientists conspiring with the national government. Chances are that, instead of calling the U.S. Army to report an alien invasion, Mr. Jones will accept the simpler explanation, get in his car, and start searching the neighborhood for the runaway dog.

Another example: Coach Wilson asks Delbert, "Why did you miss class this morning? Did you forget to set your alarm clock again?" Delbert replies, "No, honest; I meant to come to class; in fact, I was on my way, but my bicycle got a flat tire, and while I was pushing it to the garage to get the tire fixed, I tripped and sprained my ankle, so then I had to hop to the doctor's office on one foot, and the doctor gave me a shot for the pain, but the shot made me dizzy, and I fell into the duck pond in front of the clinic, and one of the ducks bit me and I had to go back into the doctor's office and get stitches, and then I had to go home to change out of my wet clothes, and by that time"—but Coach Wilson is already scowling in disbelief. He has already decided to believe the simpler explanation—that Delbert, as usual, forgot to set his alarm clock.

Like Mr. Jones and Coach Wilson, you can save yourself a great deal of worry and confusion if you remember Mr. Occam's wonderful razor: **Most of the time, the simplest explanation is the best.**

Name _____ Date _____

ASSIGNMENT: Occam's Razor

1. Have you ever heard any stories or explanations that were too complicated to believe? Can you give an example? _____

_____

_____

_____

2. What is a conspiracy? Are conspiracies common in fiction, movies, and television programs? Can you think of any examples? _____

_____

_____

_____

3. How common do you suppose conspiracies are in real life? How difficult would it be to set up a good conspiracy? _____

_____

_____

_____

_____

4. Early one stormy morning, your teacher arrives at the classroom and finds a mess: two windows are broken, and papers and other objects are strewn all over the room. How many ways can you think of to explain this situation? _____

_____

_____

_____

_____

5. Which explanation (or explanations) seems the most likely? Why? _____

_____

_____

_____

_____

PART THREE: LOGIC

14. But What Is Logic, Mr. Spock?

Fans of the original *Star Trek* television series were familiar with Mr. Spock, an alien with pointed ears and permanently raised eyebrows. Mr. Spock was forever talking about the importance of "logic" and correcting others for illogical thought and behavior—often to the annoyance of his friends, especially the passionate Dr. McCoy. Perhaps it was just as well Mr. Spock never got around to explaining what he meant by the word *logic;* his companions on the starship *Enterprise* might have walked out on his lecture.

Listening to Mr. Spock, the viewers of *Star Trek* got the clear impression that logic is important and probably vital, even for earthlings. But what, exactly, did Mr. Spock mean when he used the word *logic*?

In order to understand completely, we must return for a moment to the Greek philosopher Aristotle, who was a pioneer in the study of rhetoric (and who might have been Mr. Spock's teacher). Aristotle believed that writers and speakers rely on three methods of persuasion: he called these methods **ethos** (the appeal to ethics), **pathos** (the appeal to emotion), and **logos** (the appeal to reason). *Ethos* involves the ethical character of the writer himself. That is to say, a person who attempts to persuade others must establish that his character is good, that he knows what he is talking about, and that he is not unduly biased. For example, suppose you were to read in a magazine that cheese is the healthiest food known to man—rich in vitamins and minerals, able to add zest and energy to your life—and, incidentally, one of the tastiest snacks in the supermarket. Will you rush to the nearest grocery store and fill your shopping cart with cheese? Probably not—not after you discover that the author of the article also happens to be the owner of a cheese factory. Now the cheese-maker may have a heart of gold, but he also has good reason to be biased: the more cheese people eat, the more money he makes. You would be much more likely to buy and eat cheese if you were advised to do so by a doctor who has nothing to lose or gain from the sale of cheese. In this case, a doctor would have more *ethical appeal* than a cheese-maker.

Pathos is the appeal to emotion. Writers are often warned against becoming too emotional, but even Mr. Spock understood that emotion is an essential part of human nature. (The scripts of *Star Trek* made it clear that, even though Mr. Spock rarely let his feelings show, he loved his friends and was willing to die for them if necessary.) For all his reliance on logic, Mr. Spock would not have objected to *emotional appeal*—provided there was more to an argument than just a gush of feeling. And this is where logic enters the picture.

Logos is the *rational appeal,* the appeal to the logic and the mind. **Logic** means clear and well-organized thinking. To think logically is to draw conclusions based on evidence rather than on prejudice, superstition, senseless fear, or wishful thinking. Logic is as much a part of human nature as emotion. Some people are more logical than others, but all of us use some degree of logic every day of our lives, whether we realize it or not. Even Dr. McCoy had to think logically in order to get through medical school.

Well, you may say, it is all very well for an alien from outer space to praise logic, but the human mind is an unruly thing, full of many strange notions and whims. Is it really possible to think in an orderly way? Fortunately, Aristotle and other scholars have studied the art of clear thinking and have explained some of the rules in ways we can understand. The two main types of logic are **induction** and **deduction,** and we shall take a close look at both of them in the next few chapters.

Name _____ Date _____

ASSIGNMENT: Methods of Persuasion

Are you convinced by the following appeals? Why or why not?

1. As a major Hollywood film director, I know the best way to create a strong family life is to take the entire family to the movies at least twice a week. _____

_____

2. Take the vacation of your dreams on the Swankmore Cruise ship and discover all of your fantasies brought to life—romance, beauty, the splendor of lush sunsets, the invigorating tang of fresh sea air, the lusty aroma of lobster stew, music calling you to dance the night away—what more could you ask for? _____

_____

3. Senator Foghorn is a good family man who adores his three beautiful daughters and his faithful spaniel, Floppy. Senator Foghorn visits his elderly mother three times a week and stops to pet homeless cats whenever he passes them on the street. Shouldn't you have a kindhearted senator like Foghorn? _____

_____

4. According to major studies by the United Nations, the Salvation Army, and the Red Cross, thousands of children are going without food and medicine because of recent droughts in Africa and Asia. Can you think of any sound more heartbreaking than the cry of a hungry child? I, the Surgeon General of the United States, urge you to fight hunger and disease by sending a check to your favorite relief organization. _____

_____

5. Cliff Dunkitt, famous basketball star, urges all Americans to exercise regularly and eat nutritious meals. _____

_____

_____

PART THREE: LOGIC

15. Induction

Induction or **inductive logic** means to draw a general conclusion after examining many specific examples or pieces of evidence. Induction is **reasoning from the specific to the general.** Scientists use induction when they perform experiments in laboratories. When the rest of us use induction in our daily lives, we often call it "learning from experience."

For example, one Monday you enter Fudd's Department Store, looking for a new pair of socks. Somewhat to your surprise, no clerks or salespeople are in sight, and when Mr. Fudd finally emerges from his dark and cluttered office, he acts grumpy, as if it were highly unreasonable for you to come into his store expecting to buy something. After a twenty-minute wait, you buy your socks and walk out of the store with a shrug, thinking to yourself, "Mr. Fudd sure was in a bad mood; he must be having a terrible day." But on Friday you return to the store to buy a hat, and you discover that Mr. Fudd's bad day has apparently turned into a bad week. He snaps unpleasantly at you, and this time he keeps you waiting for half an hour. Two weeks later you go to Fudd's Department Store a third time and find a clerk at the counter, but she is chatting on the telephone with a friend, and she takes no notice of you. Mr. Fudd is in the office staring at his computer screen. He never looks up, and you leave the store without buying anything.

You talk to your friends, and they say things like, "Boy, that Fudd—what a grouch!" or "Don't ever go to Fudd's when you're in a hurry—you'll spend half an hour just trying to get somebody's attention!" Based on all these pieces of **specific evidence,** you draw the **conclusion** that Fudd's Department Store is a bad place to shop, and you take your business to a different store.

The scientist's methods are similar. Let us say that a biologist wants to determine whether or not it is dangerous to eat broccoli. He gathers two large groups of laboratory mice, and the mice in both groups receive exactly the same treatment—the same amount of sunlight and exercise, the same basic diet, and so forth—except that the mice in Group A receive food that has been specially treated with Extract of Broccoli, unlike the mice in Group B. (Because our biologist is also good at statistics, he knows how many mice to use and how much time the experiment ought to take.) Perhaps he will eventually notice the mice in Group A are sickly and a little disoriented, while the mice in Group B are thriving. He concludes that broccoli is dangerous and issues a warning to the public. Or maybe he gets the opposite result: the mice in Group A are noticeably healthier, stronger, more energetic, and better at solving mazes than the mice in Group B. He writes to a medical journal, announcing that broccoli is good for both the mind and the body. A third possibility is that the mice in Group A and Group B are equally healthy and alert. The biologist's **conclusion:** if you like broccoli, eat it, but don't expect it to transform you into an Olympian. In this case, the many mice are the specific pieces of evidence on which the scientist bases his logic.

Induction teaches us much of what we know about the world and its people. But induction, like anything else, can go all wrong and get out of control if it is used incorrectly. In the next two chapters, we shall examine some of the common problems with inductive reasoning.

Name _____ Date _____

ASSIGNMENT: Thinking About Induction

1. What sorts of things have you learned from experience? Give a few examples.

_____

_____

2. Have you ever conducted an experiment as part of a science class or club activity? If so, was inductive reasoning a part of the experiment?

_____

_____

3. You read in the newspaper that Senator Foghorn is practically certain to win re-election. But the election is almost two months away. How could anyone possibly know what the results will be?

_____

_____

4. You are horrified to learn that XYZ Television Network has decided to cancel your favorite television show. Why would the executives at XYZ do such a thing?

_____

_____

5. "Seat belts save lives!" announces the Surgeon General. How does he know?

_____

_____

6. You are invited to attend a rehearsal of the Prairie View Glee Club. When you arrive at the rehearsal hall, you find that the director is quarreling with the accompanist and many of the singers are coughing and sneezing. You also notice that groups of three and four people are sharing the same piece of music. Through an open door you can see the music library in disarray, with folders and sheets of music strewn everywhere. The rehearsal hall is uncomfortably hot, and the singers are constantly dodging the many wasps that are flying around the room. On the basis of this evidence, what will the Glee Club's next concert be like? Will you buy a ticket and plan to attend?

_____

_____

_____

PART THREE: LOGIC

16. Fallacies: Hasty Generalization, Begging the Question

Mr. Fudd's collie, Macbeth, is the biggest nuisance in town. At night, Macbeth keeps the neighbors awake with his constant barking. During the day, he chases cats, cars, people on bicycles, and mail carriers. Once, he actually bit a policeman and chased the dogcatcher up a tree. The conclusion is obvious: collies are noisy, bad-tempered brutes. No sensible person would own one unless he needed a vicious watchdog. Why would anyone go to the trouble to breed such animals, anyway?

Actually, the conclusion is far from obvious, because one piece of evidence proves almost nothing. In fact, the collie has a reputation of being somewhat aloof with strangers, but on the whole, it is a gentle creature, affectionate, and especially good with children. Mr. Fudd just happened to have bad luck with his collie—or perhaps he has been mistreating the dog and has thus driven it to viciousness.

A **fallacy** is a mistake in logic. The case of Macbeth the collie is a good example of the fallacy of **hasty generalization**—jumping to a conclusion without examining enough evidence. It is unfair to condemn all collies because of one bad example. All of us make hasty generalizations occasionally—because we're humans and not angels or aliens from the planet Vulcan—but we should try to avoid such generalizations as much as possible.

How much evidence is enough? That's a difficult question. In a few cases, one piece of evidence is almost more than enough to prove a point. A sensible person needs only one encounter with an angry skunk in order to be permanently convinced that skunks are best left alone. But by and large, it is impossible to prove something by citing one example. If you look hard enough, you can probably find one math teacher who is also a professional assassin, one football player who is terrified of mice, and one aggressive Persian cat that chases dogs out of her yard. Such examples, however, prove nothing about math teachers, football players, or Persian cats in general.

Another fallacy is **begging the question**—also a common mistake of human beings. We **beg the question** when we make statements like this: "It's time for the faculty of Madison School to abolish their absurd and unfair grading policies!" or "The taxes in Springfield are outrageously high!" Sometimes we feel that when we have made such statements, we have proven something important about grades or taxes. What we have actually done, however, is **to insist, without proof, on the truth of a statement that actually needs to be proven.** In order to demonstrate clearly that grades are unfair and taxes are too high, we would have to offer convincing evidence.

If we can avoid logical fallacies, we will be much more effective in our efforts to persuade people—especially intelligent people. We also need to understand fallacies in order to keep from being misled by faulty or dishonest arguments—after all, the world has its share of trickery and misinformation.

Name _____ Date _____

ASSIGNMENT: Logical Fallacies

1. Any sensible person can see that the principal of Prairie View High School is incompetent. Her policies are ruining the school, and she must be fired immediately. _____

_____

_____

2. I noticed Steven Sloshburg's new film, *The Trap Door,* got a good review in the *Chicago Tribune,* and Channel Ten's movie critic rated *The Trap Door* as her choice for the best movie of the summer. Joe and Judy went to see it last week, and they both said it was the most exciting movie they'd ever seen. Besides, I've always liked Steven Sloshburg's films. Let's forget about playing Monopoly tonight and go see *The Trap Door* instead. _____

_____

_____

3. Count Dracula was from Transylvania, and look what a monster he turned out to be! Nobody should trust Transylvanians. _____

_____

_____

4. Basketball star Cliff Dunkitt eats a heaping bowl of "Raisin Surprise" breakfast cereal every morning. He says, " 'Raisin Surprise' gives me the energy to play my best." Buy a box of "Raisin Surprise" today! _____

_____

_____

5. The Springfield Panthers have won their last seven games by lopsided scores. None of their players have been injured, and their next game is at home. They have an excellent chance to win. _____

_____

_____

6. Littleville is a terrible place to live. It's the dullest little town in all of Illinois. There's nothing to do in Littleville except stare at the walls. No intelligent person would live there._____

_____

_____

Part Three: Logic

17. The Notorious Post Hoc Fallacy

Senator Foghorn is re-elected in November, and several months later, when he makes his annual Memorial Day speech, he reminds his constituents how lucky they are to have such a fine leader as himself. Why, immediately after his election, the people of the state showed their confidence in Foghorn and the economy by rushing to the shopping malls in droves. Furthermore, in a recent poll, most citizens described themselves as either "very happy" or at least "contented" with their lives. The statistics speak for themselves: obviously, a vote for Senator Foghorn is a vote for prosperity, happiness, and a better life for everyone.

Well, maybe so and maybe not. Anyone who listens closely to Foghorn's speech will spot at least two examples of the famous **post hoc fallacy.** The phrase *post hoc* is a shortened version of the Latin expression *post hoc ergo propter hoc,* which means "After the fact, therefore because of the fact." In English words, the *post hoc* fallacy is the belief that if event B follows event A, then event A must have *caused* event B to happen. If people go on a shopping spree shortly after Senator Foghorn's re-election, then they must be celebrating the election returns!

Detecting the *post hoc* fallacy is a tricky business. Sometimes—often, in fact—event A really does cause event B. If a student stays up all night and then fails his tests in the morning, he may reasonably conclude that lack of sleep was at least one of the reasons for his failure. If Ms. Prissy drives her car at speeds above ninety miles an hour, nobody will be surprised when she has an accident. If Joe sneezes in my face, I will know who to blame when I catch a cold. But Senator Foghorn is deliberately trying to mislead his constituents. He surely knows (as we all do) that December follows November and that most people do their Christmas shopping in December no matter who wins the November election. And what about the results of the happiness survey? Here the senator is confusing the cause with the effect. Most social scientists believe that happy people tend to re-elect their leaders. Instead of being happy because they re-elected Foghorn, the voters probably re-elected Foghorn *because they were happy.* And what made them happy in the first place? It could have been any number of things, including the unseasonably warm weather and the fact that a native of the state had won five gold medals at the last Olympics. Senator Foghorn has gotten everything backwards.

As we have seen in Chapter Seven, cause-and-effect analysis is a useful activity, but it must be done carefully in order to work. We should all be cautious about making or believing statements about causes until we have studied all of the evidence.

Name _____ Date _____

ASSIGNMENT: Exercises in Logic

1. An unusual number of students failed their examinations in January, and Dr. Blatt, the chairman of the school board, thinks he understands why: the teachers aren't giving enough homework. He strongly urges every teacher to assign more papers, give more quizzes, and require more book reports. Has Dr. Blatt forgotten anything? Can you think of reasons—other than too little homework—why students might have difficulty with their schoolwork in the month of January? _____

_____

_____

_____

_____

_____

2. Coach Robinson is convinced that Madison Junior High School needs a soccer team, but several of his fellow teachers disagree. What sort of evidence would the coach need in order to prove the need for a soccer team—at least to the satisfaction of most people? _____

_____

_____

_____

_____

_____

3. Most people are familiar with the old saying: "Red sky at night—sailor's delight. Red sky at morning—sailor, take warning!" How accurate is this brief guide to weather prediction? How is it possible for a meteorologist to know in advance what the weather will be?

_____

_____

_____

_____

_____

PART THREE: LOGIC

18. Deduction: "Elementary, My Dear Watson!"

Deduction, the opposite of induction, means **reasoning from the general to the specific.** To use **deductive logic** means to begin with a general truth and draw a conclusion about a specific case. Sherlock Holmes, the famous fictional detective, is a genius when it comes to the art of deduction. Holmes, whose sharp eyes never miss anything, might be trying to uncover the identity of a forger of priceless manuscripts. He notices that Professor Scrabble, one of the suspects, has a callus on the third finger of his right hand. Holmes knows of nothing that could produce such a callus except the constant pressure of a pen or pencil. He therefore **deduces** that Professor Scrabble has been doing an unusual amount of writing lately—writing with a pen, not with a typewriter. Because a forger of manuscripts has to spend most of his time writing with a pen, Holmes immediately focuses his investigation on Professor Scrabble. "It's elementary!" he tells his friend and assistant, Dr. Watson. Holmes has begun with a **general** truth—that writing causes a callused third finger—and has drawn a conclusion about a **specific** individual, Professor Scrabble.

A special kind of deductive logic is the **syllogism** (SIL-uh-jiz-um). A syllogism consists of three statements: a **major premise** (the general truth), a **minor premise** (the specific case), and the **conclusion.** Many textbooks use the following example of a syllogism:

All men are mortal (*major premise*).
John is a man (*minor premise*).
Therefore, John is mortal (*conclusion*).

Few of us, if any, go around talking and thinking in perfect syllogisms. Yet all of us carry a great many major premises in our heads, and all of us use deductive logic whether we are aware of it or not. For example, if you know anything about animals, you know that angry, aggressive dogs raise their hackles and bare their fangs. One afternoon while you are taking a walk around the neighborhood, you encounter Macbeth the collie. You notice that every hair on the back of his neck is standing on end, and you also see he has drawn his lips back into a snarl. You conclude that Macbeth is in a mood to attack. You also know an angry dog is likely to chase anything that runs, so you walk away as calmly as possible, being careful to avoid eye contact with Macbeth. Your train of thought has gone something like this:

Raised hackles and bared fangs are a sure sign of an angry dog.
Macbeth is raising his hackles and baring his fangs.
Therefore, Macbeth is angry.

Angry dogs often bite.
Macbeth is angry.
Therefore, Macbeth may bite me.

Unfortunately, not all logic is this simple, and the deductive logic can be riddled with fallacies. In the next two chapters, we will look at some common problems with deductive logic.

Name _____ Date _____

ASSIGNMENT: A Little Detective Story

"Thank goodness you've come, Inspector Fizzle," Lord Whatsit cried. "I'm so grateful to you for coming all the way to Whatsit Manor on this cold day in the middle of February. Here's the problem: somebody broke into my jewelry box this morning and stole my priceless diamond tie clasp! All the doors and windows were locked at the time, and no one has entered or left the house, so the thief has to be one of three people—either the butler, the chef, or the gardener. But which one?"

Inspector Fizzle looked around Lord Whatsit's dressing room. He saw that the lock on the jewelry box had been broken, apparently with a heavy tool. On the floor he found a clump of dirt with bits of decaying leaves.

"Where are the suspects at this moment?" he asked Lord Whatsit.

"Well, the butler has been in the pantry polishing silver all morning; the chef is scrubbing the kitchen floor for the third time this week; and the gardener is packing his suitcase for a long trip."

Can you finish this story?

_____

_____

_____

_____

_____

_____

_____

_____

_____

_____

PART THREE: LOGIC

19. True and False Premises

Deduction is wonderful when it works properly, but in order for deduction to work, **the premises must be true.** False premises will not produce a true conclusion except by accident.

For example, consider the following conversation:

"I wouldn't have any more to do with Senator Foghorn than you can possibly help. The man's a crook!"

"Foghorn, a crook? Well, I've never cared much for his campaign advertisements, but how can you call him a crook?"

"Easy—he's a politician, isn't he?"

The "logic" behind this conversation goes like this:

All politicians are crooks (*major premise*).
Senator Foghorn is a politician (*minor premise*).
Therefore, Senator Foghorn is a crook (*conclusion*).

The trouble with this argument is that **the major premise is false** (and thus the conclusion is probably false, too). Anyone who is familiar with American history can give many examples of politicians who served their country well without resorting to any serious crimes.

A minor premise might also be false. Here's an example:

All vicious and evil creatures should be killed (*major premise*).
Wolves are vicious and evil (*minor premise*).
Therefore, wolves should be killed (*conclusion*).

In this argument, the **minor premise** is false, or at least highly doubtful. An expert in animal behavior would probably advise you not to approach a wild wolf and certainly not to keep a wolf as a house pet. But most intelligent people no longer think of the wolf as "evil." We have learned that wolves can be friendly and affectionate toward one another, that a wolf has his place in the grand scheme of nature, and that, although wolves can cause problems, they are on the whole useful and attractive animals. A person who kills a wolf has not necessarily done the world a favor.

All of us have our favorite premises—all math courses are dull, all beautiful girls are conceited, cats are treacherous, straight-A students are boring people, scientists are mad and evil, newspapers always print the truth, mules are dumb. But in order to avoid reaching false conclusions, we should sometimes ask whether premises are really true.

Name _____ Date _____

ASSIGNMENT: Exercises in Logic

Evaluate the logic in the following passages. Do you find any of these arguments convincing?

1. According to all the reference books, an English bulldog makes an excellent pet for small children. Mr. Jones has three small sons at home; if he wants a dog, he should consider getting an English bulldog. _____

_____

_____

2. It's true—black cats really do bring bad luck! Last week, a black cat crossed my path, and the very next day I wrecked my car. I wouldn't have a black cat in my house for a million dollars! _____

_____

_____

3. I'm really looking forward to meeting Mary. She must be nice; after all, she was born and raised in a good, old-fashioned, all-American small town. _____

_____

_____

4. Of course Dr. Evans is a bore. He teaches history. He spends all of his time reading dull history books; how could he possibly have anything interesting to say?_____

_____

_____

5. My car didn't drive itself out of the parking lot; somebody must have stolen it. I'm going to call the police. _____

_____

_____

6. Let's kill that bat before it bites us and drinks our blood! _____

_____

_____

_____

PART THREE: LOGIC

20. "All Animals are Kangaroos!" —Invalid and Equivocal Logic

When logic is twisted out of shape, an argument is said to be **invalid**. A **valid** syllogism follows a precise pattern:

All cats have fur.
Puff is a cat.
Therefore, Puff has fur.

So far, so good, but if the words of the syllogism are rearranged, a strange conclusion is the result:

All cats have fur.
Puff has fur.
Therefore, Puff is a cat.

It is easy to see the illogic of this example. All sorts of animals have fur, including dogs, beavers, monkeys, rabbits, chipmunks, bears—the list is long. The fact that Puff has fur is no proof that Puff is a cat. One might just as well argue that because every kangaroo is an animal, then every animal must be a kangaroo.

Not all invalid arguments are so obvious. Suppose you are shopping in your favorite mall, and you notice a bearded man who is wearing the most shabby, dirty clothes you have ever seen in your life. You know that tramps wear threadbare clothes, and you suspect that a tramp in the mall must be intending to steal something, so you decide to notify the security guard, because:

All tramps wear shabby clothes.
The bearded man is wearing shabby clothes.
Therefore, the bearded man is a tramp.

As you can see, we are back to the "all animals are kangaroos" position. Yes, tramps wear old clothes, but so do lots of other people—including perhaps an artist who is working on an oil painting and doesn't want to ruin his best suit. Keep an eye on the bearded man, and if he goes into the crafts store and starts buying canvases and paint brushes, he is more likely to be an artist than a tramp.

Equivocation (ee-kwiv-uh-KAY-shun) is the fallacy (or the deceptive practice) of **changing the definition of an important word in the middle of an argument.** Thus Delbert argues that neither he nor anyone else should be required to study English, because the English book has a long section on argument, and no one should be *forced* to argue— such a distasteful thing to do, shouting and shaking fists at people! Delbert is a man of peace;

41

he shouldn't have to take English if he doesn't want to!

It is doubtful that Delbert can make his point stick, because he is obviously **equivocating**—using the word *argument* in two different senses at once. As we have seen, an argument can be a verbal fight or quarrel, or it can simply be an attempt to persuade, with no fist-shaking or ill will of any kind.

By now you should be getting an idea of how logic works, though. Perhaps you can also see that logic is invaluable in many situations. Remember Inspector Fizzle and his three suspects—the butler, the chef, and the gardener? Which of them is the thief? By making a close study of the dressing room, the inspector has learned that the thief smashed a lock with a heavy tool and that the thief tracked dirt on the floor. Logic suggests that a chef would have heavy tools—but Lord Whatsit's chef must be obsessed with cleanliness if he scrubs the floor three times a week; this chef would never wear dirty shoes into the house. The butler also seems to be preoccupied with cleanliness; neither he nor the chef are likely suspects. The dirt on the floor contains fragments of decaying leaves, and gardeners use leaves as mulch or fertilizer. Another suspicious thing: unless the gardener has suddenly been called out of town on an emergency, isn't it strange that he is packing for a long trip in the middle of February? Most people take their vacations at Christmas or in the summer. Is it possible that the gardener is planning to take the stolen diamonds and flee to Mexico? Such evidence might not convince a jury, but it would certainly convince Inspector Fizzle to keep a close eye on that gardener just in case he tries to escape.

Name _____   Date _____

ASSIGNMENT: Logical Fallacies

Try writing a piece of *terrible logic*—filled with false premises, *post hoc* fallacies, hasty generalizations, and any other fallacies you can come up with.

_____

_____

_____

_____

_____

_____

_____

_____

_____

PART FOUR: MORE FALLACIES AND PROBLEMS

21. "If We Can Send a Man to the Moon, We Can Make Bulletproof Stockings!"

It was exciting to be alive during the days of the Apollo Program. What a privilege to watch Neil Armstrong live on television when he became the first human being to set foot on the Moon! And who can forget the spectacular, fiery rocket launches and the extraordinary courage and resourcefulness of the *Apollo 13* crew? The Apollo program was one of the proudest accomplishments in human history.

Oddly enough, however, the Apollo Moon landings were the occasion for a great deal of grumbling. Many people reasoned that if man is smart enough to fly to the Moon, then he surely must be smart enough to solve the problems of day-to-day living right here on planet Earth. So why hasn't man solved his problems yet? Obviously, because he is lazy, irresponsible, and childish; he would rather play at space exploration than make serious efforts to create a better world. Many of the grumbles went like this: "If we can send a man to the Moon, we can make stockings that don't run!", "If we can send a man to the Moon, we can find a cure for the common cold!", or "If we can send a man to the Moon, we can solve the problem of world hunger!"

No doubt these grumblers had good intentions, but they were committing the logical fallacy of **non sequitur** (non SEK-wi-ter), a Latin phrase meaning "It does not follow." Non sequitur is a fallacy of deduction in which **the conclusion does not follow from the premises.** Here are two examples:

All cats have fur.
Puff is a cat.
Therefore, Puff is a long-haired silver tabby.

Good students should be rewarded.
I am a good student.
Therefore, my grandmother should buy me a new motorcycle.

It is easy to see what's wrong with these two syllogisms. In the first example, we can deduce that Puff has fur, but neither the major nor the minor premise tell us anything about the color, length, or pattern of Puff's fur. (Of course, if we also knew Puff was descended from a long line of silver tabby Persian cats, we would not be surprised when Puff also turned out to be a silver tabby Persian.) In the second example, the conclusion has almost no connection with the premises. The usual "reward" for a good student is high grades—but not a new motorcycle, alas.

And what about the indestructible stockings, the cure for the common cold, and the solution to world hunger? Well, for one thing, the problem of hunger has many causes, including the weather: famines are often caused by droughts and floods. And because man has little control over floods and droughts, it is illogical to compare Moon exploration to famine. We might as well argue, "If we can send a man to the Moon, we can control the weather!" The so-called "common cold" comes in so many varieties that it resists a single, simple cure. Stockings, by their very nature, must be soft, semitransparent, and highly flexible; is it really feasible to make such garments out of steel thread? One might as well argue, "If we can send a man to the Moon, we can train spiders to spin bulletproof webs!"

Name _____ Date _____

ASSIGNMENT: Avoiding Fallacies

You are campaigning for a position on your school's student council (president, vice president, secretary, treasurer, historian, editor of the newspaper, parliamentarian, entertainment chairperson, poet laureate, captain of the drill team, student librarian, or head of the cheering squad).

1. Decide which office would best suit your talents, experience, and interests.

_____

2. What are your qualifications for this position? List three or four of them.

_____

_____

_____

3. Write a campaign speech in which you describe your specific qualifications for office. Try to avoid fallacies such as *begging the question* and such *non sequiturs* as "I work hard as a member of the tennis team; therefore I would make a good president for the student council."

_____

_____

_____

_____

_____

_____

_____

_____

PART FOUR: MORE FALLACIES AND PROBLEMS

22. The False Dilemma and the Slippery Slope

Mr. Jones goes to a meeting of the Springfield City Council to complain about the many potholes in the streets near his house. Because he is a serious and thoughtful man, he has chosen to prepare a short speech rather than to speak whatever words come to his mind during the meeting. But halfway through his speech, Councilman Bluff cuts him off in mid-sentence: "I'm sick of listening to whiners like you! All you ever do is complain, complain, complain! Look, you're lucky to live in a great city like Springfield, and if you don't like it here, you can just move somewhere else!" (In other words, *Springfield!—love it or leave it.*) Mr. Jones leaves the meeting dejected but unconvinced. On his way home, he steps in a pothole, stumbles, sprains his ankle, and has to limp back to his house and soak his foot. Should he start packing his bags to leave town?

The flaw in Councilman Bluff's logic is the **fallacy of the false dilemma** (also known as the **two extremes fallacy** or the **excluded middle**). Much as we humans like to talk about "good" and "bad" or "right" and "wrong," life rarely presents us with two and only two clear-cut choices. We can react to a town or city in many different ways, and probably most of us have conflicting feelings about our home towns. We say such things as, "I'm from Littleville; it's kind of a slow, dull village, especially in the summer, and the shopping area is starting to look pretty shabby—but the people are really friendly; they'd do anything for you." And even the most beautiful and beloved city could probably be improved in at least one way. Certainly it is possible to love Springfield and hate potholes.

A similar fallacy is the so-called **slippery slope** argument. This fallacy is appealing to the sort of person who sees danger lurking everywhere. Some examples: If the mayor of Springfield purchases an abstract painting instead of a portrait or landscape to hang in City Hall, he'll start a dreadful trend; pretty soon all of the municipal buildings will be filled with ugly modern art—"sculptures" made of oil cans and rusty nails and paintings that look like ink blots—and there will be no beauty left in all of Springfield. If we allow the principal of Madison School to install a candy vending machine in the cafeteria, we'll be encouraging bad habits in our children; soon they'll be spending so much money on candy that they won't be able to buy textbooks, and they'll be gorging themselves on unwholesome snacks instead of eating healthy food, until they grow too soft to play sports, too sluggish to study, and too fat to get up from their chairs!

In the musical comedy *The Music Man,* Professor Harold Hill plans to cheat the people of River City, and he uses a slippery slope argument to advance his scheme. In the amusing song "Ya Got Trouble," he tells the townspeople all about the evils of playing pool: allow a pool table in your community, he says, and the next thing you know, your children will start reading trashy novels and using vile words like "swell." Next they'll begin drinking beer on the sly, then gambling at horse races, and finally dancing the night away at wild parties—going to ruin generally. The solution: Professor Hill will organize a wonderful marching band that will lure the children away from the dangerous pool table. Actually, "Professor Hill" is a fake, a confidence man who can't even read music. The marching band exists only in his imagination.

45

In spite of his faults, Harold Hill is basically a kind and endearing man. Eventually he falls in love with the town librarian, gives up his life of crime, and presumably lives happily ever after as a beloved and respected citizen of River City. Not all tricksters are so good-hearted, however, so a wise person should always be alert for logical fallacies.

Name _____ Date _____

ASSIGNMENT: An Exercise in Super-Salesmanship

1. Watch a video of *The Music Man* (or listen to a recording of the original Broadway cast). Pay particular attention to the song entitled "Ya Got Trouble." How does Professor Hill use faulty logic to get people's attention? In general, how logical are the people of River City? Do they remind you of any people you know? _____

_____

_____

_____

2. Study some real advertisements in magazines and newspapers and on television. Can you find any examples of logical fallacies? _____

_____

_____

_____

3. Imagine you are a salesperson. (*You* can decide what to sell—cars, hot dogs, swimming lessons, anything.) Can you write a "sales pitch" similar to the one used by Harold Hill?

_____

_____

_____

_____

_____

_____

_____

46

PART FOUR: MORE FALLACIES AND PROBLEMS

23. Arguments From Authority: "More Doctors Eat Broccoli"

The pleasant-looking man on the television screen says, "I'm a plumber, but when I have a splitting headache, I can't get any work done. So I talked to my daughter, Elvira, who's a doctor, and she said to take Head-eeze tablets to relieve my pain. I followed her good advice, and now I'm working at top speed again. There's not a single clogged drain in town—thanks to me and Head-eeze."

Well, one might suppose that a doctor's recommendation is a good enough reason to try Head-eeze. After all, a doctor has to study for years; Elvira surely knows her way around a drug store, doesn't she? But before you rush out to buy a year's supply of Head-eeze, notice there are two problems with the plumber's argument. First, chances are that Dr. Elvira is a fictional character, the invention of a writer who specializes in advertisements. Fictional characters make poor medical experts—would you buy a headache remedy from Captain Hook or Lex Luthor? But even if Elvira is real, what is her recommendation actually worth? After all, she is only one doctor out of many, and doctors may disagree about headache remedies. Furthermore, we know little about Elvira's true qualifications. She might be an excellent doctor; she might be a mediocre doctor; she might have cheated her way through medical school; she might be a doctor of psychology rather than medicine; she might even be a horse doctor, for all we know. Chances are that Head-eeze tablets are neither better nor worse than any of the other pain relievers on the market. The tale of Dr. Elvira is a good example of the fallacy of **argument from authority.**

In this complicated world, everyone has to rely on the advice of experts occasionally; nobody has either the time or the ability to be his own doctor, lawyer, mechanic, computer programmer, and movie critic. But a sensible person will be careful about which "experts" he trusts. If he needs to hire a mechanic, for example, he doesn't just pick a name out of the Yellow Pages—not if he cares about his car and his pocketbook. Instead, he asks his friends and neighbors to recommend someone who is honest and reliable.

All of us have heard statements such as these: "Studies show broccoli is the most nutritious of all vegetables.", "Experts say eating broccoli builds strong muscles.", "Boffo the Lumberjack says, 'I have the strength of ten men because I eat my broccoli every day!'", and "More doctors eat broccoli!". (How many doctors is "more"? More than what? And how much broccoli do they eat, anyway?) We should be at least a little skeptical of such claims whenever we encounter them, either in advertisements or elsewhere. Enjoy the cartoon adventures of Boffo the Lumberjack if you like, but don't get the idea that he is some kind of infallible authority.

One should also be skeptical of **mass authority**—such statements as "They say that broccoli is filled with vitamins" or "Everyone knows broccoli is nutritious" or "It's common knowledge that broccoli builds strong bones." "Common knowledge" has often turned out to be ignorance. A few centuries ago, "everyone" knew that the earth was the center of the universe, that witches should be burned at the stake, and that cats were devils in disguise.

Of course, "everyone" often shows great wisdom. As E.B. White once noted, democracy is based on the idea that "everyone" is right more than half of the time, and democracy seems to work better than any other form of government. Nevertheless, in many fields—such as biology and computer science, for example—"everyone" is no more an expert than Boffo the Lumberjack.

Name _____ Date _____

ASSIGNMENT: Using Logic

Evaluate the following arguments:

1. Why should I feel sorry for people who can't find jobs? The way I see it, in this world either a man works hard and pulls his weight or he's a lazy bum. _____

_____

2. Fizzle-Cola!—the favorite soft drink of the modern generation! _____

_____

3. I have served my country honorably in the army and have won medals for bravery. Therefore I deserve to be elected President of the United States. _____

_____

4. It's a bad idea for Madison School to have a student council. If we let the kids have an election and pick their own officers, pretty soon they'll expect to run the whole school, and the next thing you know, they'll be taking over the principal's office and rioting in the hallways. _____

_____

5. You're crazy to vote for Senator Foghorn. Everybody knows he's a crook. _____

_____

6. I read in the *Littleville Daily News* that purple and pink will be a fashionable combination this spring. So I'm going straight to the store to buy some purple skirts and pink blouses.

_____

7. If you care about hunger, poverty, and disease, it is your duty to send money to Heartstring Charities. After all, if you're not part of the solution, you're part of the problem. _____

_____

_____

PART FOUR: MORE FALLACIES AND PROBLEMS

24. Ignoring the Question

"Senator Foghorn, if you're re-elected, what will you do to protect out national symbol, the majestic bald eagle?" a reporter asks at a press conference.

The senator hesitates a moment before he replies. "That's an excellent question, sir, and I'm glad you asked. The way I see it, in order to protect wild creatures like the bald eagle, American society must return to basic family values. Parents need to spend time with their children and teach them the importance of patriotism, hard work, and respect for all living things."

The senator's answer is bound to be pleasing to most members of the audience: after all, no reasonable person can be opposed to the idea of parents spending time with their children. Notice, however, that Senator Foghorn has deftly changed the subject on the reporter. "Family values" have nothing to do with protecting eagles—not unless the senator actually believes that strong, loving families are guaranteed to turn out patriotic, eagle-loving American citizens. Besides, it is one thing to love eagles and quite another matter to come up with a workable plan to protect them. Senator Foghorn, who obviously doesn't want to talk about eagles today, is using a tactic known as **ignoring the question**.

But why is the senator so reluctant to answer the reporter's question directly, instead fudging around with talk of "family values?" We don't really know, but probably Senator Foghorn doesn't want to admit he really has no idea how to protect the eagles. Or perhaps his record on eagle protection is shaky: maybe he has voted against every eagle-protection act. Maybe he even shoots at the eagles who roost in the trees near his riverside cabin.

In Clarence Day's humorous book *Life with Father,* Mr. Day insists that his son take violin lessons, even though the boy hates the violin, has no musical talent, and is almost tone deaf. Mr. Day himself is deaf to every reasonable argument. The violin is the noblest instrument ever invented, he says, and anyone who has a chance to take violin lessons should be grateful. Mr. Day is ignoring the issue, which was not the nobility of the violin, but the very different question of whether a tone-deaf child should be forced to take music lessons that he loathes.

An honest speaker or writer will address issues directly instead of ignoring them. If you want to win respect, remember to focus on the issues—and beware of people who try to change the subject.

Name _____ Date _____

ASSIGNMENT: Reading Report

Read the chapter entitled "The Noblest Instrument" in Clarence Day's *Life with Father*.

1. How many problems does Father cause when he insists that his son must learn to play the violin? _____

_____

_____

2. As a result of the violin lessons, Father becomes involved in several disagreements: with Mother, with the violin teacher, and with the neighbors. How does Father answer their arguments? _____

_____

_____

3. How would you describe Father's logic? _____

_____

_____

4. The violin teacher feels like a failure because he earns less money than Father does. Is the violin teacher being logical? Can you think of any "successful" people who earn little money? _____

_____

_____

_____

5. Clarence Day writes that Father was never "insidious," but that he liked to discuss matters from an "impregnable" angle. What does Day mean? Consult a dictionary if necessary.

_____

_____

_____

6. In spite of his talent for debate, Father is eventually defeated. Why? How could he have handled the matter differently? _____

_____

_____

_____

PART FOUR: MORE FALLACIES AND PROBLEMS

25. Analogy: Its Use and Abuse

Dr. Tribble, a retired minister, is the laughingstock of his neighborhood because he spends much of his time in his basement laboratory, where he is trying to build a time machine. Peculiar though he may be, Dr. Tribble is not stupid. He knows perfectly well that his neighbors—*and* his long-suffering wife—*and* his three embarrassed children—consider him a little crazy, but he has an answer that always silences his critics. "Well," he says patiently, "they laughed at Columbus; they laughed at Fulton; they laughed at the Wright brothers."

Dr. Tribble is arguing by **analogy**. That is, he reasons that if two things are alike in some ways, they will be alike in other ways too. Simply put, his argument goes like this: Columbus, Fulton, and the Wrights attempted to launch revolution in travel; they met with ridicule; they triumphed in the end. Like them, I am trying to accomplish a revolution in travel; like them, I am meeting with ridicule; like them, I will triumph in the end.

There are two things to remember about analogies: First, an **analogy proves nothing**; it can only illustrate. Second, an analogy is fair *only if the things being compared are truly similar*. Dr. Tribble's argument fails partly because there is a significant difference between himself and the great pioneering innovators like Columbus, Fulton, and the Wrights, who actually knew something abut their chosen fields. Dr. Tribble, in his younger days, was no doubt a good minister—patient, kind, dedicated—but he knows nothing about physics, about time, or about any other branch of science. Besides, even if some geniuses were ridiculed, we have no reason to conclude that everyone who is ridiculed is a genius. As astronomer Carl Sagan once wrote, "They laughed at Columbus, they laughed at Fulton, they laughed at the Wright brothers, but they also laughed at Bozo the Clown."

Father, whom we met in the previous chapter, was also using a false analogy when he demanded that his son learn to play the violin. Because Father was talented at music, he assumed that his son would, of course, share that talent: *Like father, like son!* But the analogy is clearly false: a son's heredity differs greatly from that of his father. Sometimes a son inherits his father's talents, but not always.

Another problem with analogy is that sometimes two things appear to be similar, almost identical, but they may still have significant differences that are not at all obvious. So, for example, the principal of Littleville High School might argue that Littleville should launch a soccer program similar to the one in the town of Fudge River. Just look at the two towns— Littleville and Fudge River are almost identical in size; both of them are located on the prairies of Illinois; they have exactly the same number of high school students; the two towns are almost mirror images of each other! And the soccer program at Fudge River has been a huge success; it has increased school spirit and morale among students and faculty alike, and it has brought prestige and honor to both the school and the town. A soccer program is just what Littleville needs to lift it out of those small-town doldrums! But the principal is overlooking one thing: the population of Fudge River includes five millionaires who also happen to be soccer fanatics and who have made generous donations to the high school soccer program. Littleville, on the other hand, boasts only one millionaire, and he is a hermit and a miser who leaves his house only to go to city council meetings and complain about his taxes. Quite simply, Fudge River has money to spend on a soccer program, and Littleville does not. This fact does not mean Littleville should give up the idea of soccer altogether—money isn't everything, after all—but the principal should at least be aware that comparisons with Fudge River are misleading.

Even though an analogy is not the same thing as logical proof, it can be enlightening. Benjamin Franklin, who was famous for his sense of humor, once said that fish and guests start to smell after three days. This brief comparison is both forceful and amusing, and for over two centuries Franklin's words have served as a useful warning to houseguests who might overstay their welcome. But Franklin was wise; he surely knew there was a big difference between a human being and a rotting fish. Some houseguests have valid reasons to stay longer than three days. In fact, if the guest has come to care for a seriously ill relative, he or she might have to stay for three weeks or even three months.

In short, be careful with analogies. Useful as they are, they can also be tricky and misleading.

Name _____ Date _____

ASSIGNMENT: Problems in Logic

Evaluate the following arguments:

1. Don't change horses in the middle of the stream! Re-elect Joseph Q. Foghorn to the Senate! _____

_____

2. The advanced and elegant Synchrotex watch is Europe's favorite timepiece. _____

_____

3. Every boy and girl in America should learn how to play basketball. After all, basketball is the most exciting sport known to man, and it is rapidly becoming one of the most popular sports in the world. _____

_____

4. My sister Laura has a face and figure just like Nancy Kerrigan. I bet she'll make a terrific ice skater. _____

_____

5. It may be true that, in order to build the new Springfield Amusement Park and Shoppers' Paradise, we'll have to cut down hundreds of trees and destroy the habitat of the endangered ring-tailed chattering sparrow. But, after all, you can't make an omelet without breaking some eggs. _____

_____

PART FOUR: MORE FALLACIES AND PROBLEMS

26. The Trouble With Statistics

Numbers are often essential pieces of evidence. If I want to buy a van, for example, I would be smart to study the figures and the statistics before I make a trip to the dealer's showroom. How much do vans usually cost? If I buy the glossy new "Thunderbolt" van, will I be getting a good bargain for my money? Which vans have the best safety records? If I buy one of the larger vans, how many miles can I expect to drive on a gallon of gas? How often will I have to take my van to the shop for repairs, and how much will those repairs probably cost? What will my van be worth four years from now, and ten years from now? I must find the answers to these questions if I want to be a smart shopper.

At times, numbers seem almost magical. Words have no such magic—most of us know words can be used in misleading ways. But numbers are so scientific, so objective, so completely reliable—as reliable as the sum of two plus two. Is it possible for statistics to be misleading?

Unfortunately, yes, and people use misleading statistics every day—sometimes deliberately, sometimes unconsciously. Take the case of Dr. Blatt, the president of the school board. The members of the local Parent-Teacher Association, ever devoted to the good of their school system, decide to conduct an evaluation of Dr. Blatt's work, and so they mail a survey to all parents. Two weeks later, the chairperson of the PTA, Ms. Quiggle—who, by the way, is planning to oppose Dr. Blatt in the next election—announces the result in an ominous tone of voice: Fully three-fourths of the respondents consider Dr. Blatt an incompetent bungler. Obviously, Dr. Blatt should be thrown out of office!—and so, probably, should the rest of the Board of Education, who have put up with his blundering and never raised a protest.

What Ms. Quiggle doesn't mention is that only eight people returned the survey, and only six of those people expressed unhappiness with Dr. Blatt. Six voters is too small a sample to prove much of anything. And what of the many citizens who failed to return the form—who threw it away or let it languish underneath a pile of bills? It's impossible to know what these people were thinking, but probably most of them had few complaints about Dr. Blatt and therefore saw no compelling reason to fill out the form, slap a stamp on it, and rush it to the post office. (Note to Ms. Quiggle: the meaning of the numbers *could actually be the opposite of what it seems*—most people are satisfied with Dr. Blatt's performance and see no reason to vote him out of office. Perhaps Ms. Quiggle should change her plans and run for sheriff instead.)

Or consider the case of Slidewell Ski Resort. Since it opened fifty years ago, Slidewell has seen a noticeable increase in all kinds of injuries and accidents. Obviously, Slidewell Resort is a dangerous place to take a vacation; in fact, the place ought to be shut down because of unsafe practices—but wait! Fifty years ago, there were fewer people in the world, and hence fewer people at ski resorts—and, of course, there were fewer skiing injuries! Slidewell is probably no more dangerous than any of the neighboring resorts.

How would you like to work at Scrooge Paper Clip Company? The employees of Scrooge Paper Clips earn an average of $37,500 a year. What a wonderful place to work, and what a generous man Mr. Scrooge is!—or is he? Actually, Mr. Scrooge has five employees who each earn a measly salary of $5,000 a year, while Mr. Scrooge pays himself a generous salary of $200,000 a year. You can do the arithmetic: $5,000 times five equals $25,000; plus $200,000 equals $225,000; divided by six equals a glorious average of $37,500. Always look sharp when you see the word *average,* and don't send a resume to Scrooge Paper Clips unless you want to work long hours for little money.

Dr. Bunion, the noted foot doctor, announces to a television reporter that 95 percent of Americans suffer from painful corns. Such a sad statistic, you think, and such a sorry state of foot-care in this country; millions of Americans limping and hobbling to work each day, smiling bravely through their pain. But think again: How could Dr. Bunion possibly have learned his information? Probably he conducted a study of his own patients—*who would never have come to Dr. Bunion in the first place if their feet were healthy and normal.* Dr. Bunion's survey was bound to produce misleading results, because his patients are not typical of Americans in general.

According to a recent article in the *Bulletin of Madison Junior High School,* "the average Madison graduate, class of 1966, owns a three-story, five-bedroom home, has four late-model cars in his driveway and a swimming pool in the back yard, and spends fifteen days in Hawaii every December." Well, three cheers for dear old Madison! She must be a wonderful school if her graduates can afford to live so well. But how could the editor of the *Bulletin* possibly know so much about the lifestyles of Madison alumni? It turns out he simply asked the people who attended his class reunion. How many of these people told him the truth, and how many were just bragging? We don't know, and neither does the editor.

The point is not that all numbers are false and misleading, but that statistical evidence is no more perfect than anything else in this world. Use statistics, yes, but use them with care. And remember that numbers are just numbers, not magical messages from an infallible wizard.

Name _____   Date _____

ASSIGNMENT: Problems With Statistics

How many problems can you find with this argument?

The numbers are frightening and shocking. During the past 25 years, crime has risen sharply in the streets of Springfield. According to a recent survey, 75 percent of citizens revealed they are afraid to leave their homes after dark. Crime is expensive: the average house burglar stole $20,000 worth of cash and valuables last year alone. What can you do to stop this crime wave? You can let your voice be heard! Vote for Jane Quiggle—your candidate for sheriff!

_____

_____

_____

_____

_____

PART FOUR: MORE FALLACIES AND PROBLEMS

27. Writing the Persuasive Essay

Now that you have studied logic and persuasion, the time has come for you to write a persuasive essay of your own. Such a task is never easy: you will need to assemble enough evidence to make your case, and you will need to avoid obvious logical fallacies. The effort is worthwhile, however, because the ability to think clearly and use evidence convincingly will serve you well in any field of work and any area of life.

Remember that a good argument, like any piece of good writing, must be organized. It is never enough just to complain or to pour your emotions out on paper. Your readers must be able to follow your argument, point by point, without getting lost or confused. The following series of steps will guide you as you prepare your essay.

ASSIGNMENT: Writing the Persuasive Essay

1. What do you believe in? What beliefs do you wish people would share with you? Try to list several. _____

_____

_____

2. Choose one of your beliefs as the subject of your essay. (Example: *The music program at Madison School is important enough to deserve more money from the school budget.*)

_____

3. What kind of evidence would help you prove your point? (Examples: *the number of people in the choir, band, jazz band, and orchestra; the number of people who attend concerts; the number of graduates who become professional musicians; the cost of sheet music and new instruments; statements from people who enjoy music.*) _____

_____

_____

4. Where can you find this information? (Examples: *Talk to the choir and band directors, read catalogs of musical instruments, ask the band's historian to show you the official scrapbook.*) _____

_____

_____

Name _____ Date _____

5. What evidence have you gained from personal experience? (Example: *Singing in the choir taught me self-confidence and helped me understand the importance of being reliable—appearing at every rehearsal, always on time.*) _____

_____

_____

_____

6. Will you need to look up any material in the library? (Example: *Perhaps find a good book about successful music programs for public schools.*) _____

_____

_____

7. What objections might be raised to your argument? (Example: *Music is not important to me; I'm going to be a lawyer. Why should my parents pay tax money to support a music program that doesn't involve me?*) _____

_____

_____

_____

8. How can you answer these objections? (Example: *Lawyers go to football games and dances, and they will enjoy these activities more if the marching bands and the dance bands play their music in tune.*) _____

_____

_____

_____

9. After studying your evidence, decide on your three or four most important points:

_____

_____

_____

_____

_____

10. Can you support these points with evidence? How?

_____

_____

_____

_____

_____

11. Write your essay on your own paper. **Good Luck!**

PART FIVE: PROPAGANDA

28. What Is Propaganda?

During the 1950s and '60s, when many Americans lived in fear of war with Communist Russia, we used to hear a great deal about the evils of "communist propaganda." Nobody bothered to explain exactly what *propaganda* was, but it sounded like a particularly sinister kind of lie that could subvert and enslave the mind. Propaganda was evil, bad for people, and bad for the world.

Today the communist empire no longer exists, and propaganda no longer looms quite so large and dark in our thoughts. Nevertheless, we would do well not to forget about propaganda altogether, because it exists everywhere, not just in communist regimes, and even if we no longer regard it as a force of darkness, it still bears watching.

What is propaganda? Dictionaries may differ on the exact definition, but many people would agree that propaganda has the following characteristics:

1. Propaganda is usually an organized effort. That is, you probably can't create real propaganda all by yourself, working like a mad scientist in the solitude of your own basement. To launch a good propaganda campaign, you would need several people— maybe thousands of people—working together.

2. Propaganda appeals to the emotions rather than to the mind. A good propagandist wants to arouse pity, fear, anger, pride, or patriotic fervor, but he is not interested in logic. In many cases, the last thing he wants is for people to use their brains.

3. The goal of propaganda is action and commitment. The propagandist wants you to do more than simply nod your head in agreement. He wants you to send money, vote for a candidate, buy a product, join an organization, carry a protest sign, or maybe even join him in an attempt to overthrow a government.

Thus, for example, if you were to write a letter to your school's newspaper, arguing for the abolition of grades, you would merely be expressing your own opinion, not writing propaganda. But suppose you formed an organization called the committee to Stamp Out Grades (SOG). And suppose that SOG started printing a highly emotional newsletter, complete with photographs of young boys and girls with hollow cheeks and sunken eyes— young people cut down in the bloom of youth, driven to the brink of insanity because of society's pressure to get and keep good grades. Then you would definitely be using propaganda.

Is propaganda bad? The answer depends on the propagandist's cause and on how truthful or deceptive he is. Some people believe that every piece of propaganda is a lie. They may have a good point; however, modern life would be difficult without propaganda, which includes most advertising, most political campaigning, many appeals for charity, and even—sometimes—your own education. If the Springfield Humane Society were to launch a campaign to raise money for a new animal shelter, their brochures might well feature heart-rending photographs of sick and starving puppies. This sort of propaganda is well-intentioned and probably harmless (although even here there is an element of deception; logic might tell us that Springfield needs a new hospital or school more than it needs an animal shelter). Still, for better or worse, the Springfield Humane Society would be dealing in propaganda.

Because propaganda is so common in our society, every citizen should learn how it works and be able to recognize it in order to keep from being fooled, cheated, and manipulated.

Name _____ Date _____

ASSIGNMENT: Thinking About Propaganda

1. Study a recent issue of a newspaper or magazine. How many examples of propaganda do you see? List them. Bring the best example to school for a presentation in class.

_____

_____

_____

2. Does propaganda play a part in the life of your school? Can you think of examples?

_____

_____

_____

3. Have you ever been helped because of a propaganda campaign? Explain.

_____

_____

_____

4. What kinds of harm might be caused by propaganda?

_____

_____

_____

5. Is lying always a bad thing? Is it possible to accomplish something good by telling a lie?

_____

_____

_____

_____

PART FIVE: PROPAGANDA

29. Name-Calling, Glittering Generalities

In order to arouse people's emotions and cloud their minds, every propagandist depends on a bag of tricks known as **propaganda devices.** Two of the most common are **name-calling** and **glittering generalities.**

Name-calling and glittering generalities are effective because most words have **connotations** in addition to their literal meanings. That is to say, a word can arouse emotions that may have little to do with its definition in the dictionary. On the literal level, for example, a *poet* is nothing more than a man or woman who writes poetry—but many people also think of poets as sissified, impractical, and dangerously foolish. A *politician* is somebody who runs for office or accepts appointments to government jobs—but most of us half-suspect that all politicians are corrupt. Some people, when they hear the word *scientist,* immediately think of the long-haired, wild-eyed character who has become familiar to all of us in horror movies and in films such as *Back to the Future.* Every good propagandist quickly learns how to manipulate people by using the connotations of words.

The device of *name-calling* means exactly what it says: the propagandist uses demeaning or scary-sounding words to turn his audience against some person, idea, or practice. During the 1950s and '60s, when the Cold War was at its height, the label "communist" was just about the scariest word in the entire dictionary. Therefore, all sorts of people accused their opponents of being "communists" or "commie-lovers" or of being "soft on Communism," or of having "communist sympathies." Today, if a propagandist can't find enough people who are still afraid of communists, he needn't despair; there are plenty of other bad names left. Our propagandist can use such terms as "socialist," "radical," "hidebound conservative," "atheist," "hopelessly old-fashioned," "liar," "stupid," "secular humanist," "bleeding heart," "racist," "sexist," or "Neanderthal." If his opponent supports a plan to hire a team of school nurses, the propagandist can ridicule the idea as "kiddy care," "the band-aid boondoggle," or the "nanny bonanza."

Thus, Senator Foghorn exclaims, "My opponent is not only a liar, he's a reckless and a stupid liar!" But don't expect the Senator to bring forth any evidence—to point out any specific lies his opponent has told or any reckless and stupid things his opponent has actually done. The last thing Senator Foghorn wants is for people to take a hard, close look at the evidence. He just wants to scare them or anger them with the words "liar," "stupid," and "reckless."

The opposite of name-calling is the *glittering generality.* To use this device, the propagandist thinks of words that make people feel happy, comfortable, or proud. Then he applies these words to himself or to his favorite cause or idea. Today, the expression "family values" has become such an attractive glittering generality that every politician tries to work it into his speeches. Other glittering expressions include "the American way of life," "the American dream," "the Moral Majority," "our national heritage," "the ideals of the Founding Fathers," "the common man," "truth," "creativity," "justice," "fairness," and "freedom." So Senator Foghorn assures his constituents, "I believe in justice for the common man, and I stand solidly for freedom." Well, good for Senator Foghorn—but freedom to do what, exactly? Freedom from what? Just who is the "common man," and why is he demanding "justice?" Don't expect the Senator to tell us. All he knows is that whenever he speaks the words "freedom" and "justice," his audience bursts into applause.

Of course, a good political speech can be fun, and there's no harm in enjoying it. But after the applause has died down, we can all save ourselves from being deceived if we take a minute to think: Where was the evidence? And what do those vile-sounding names and glittery phrases really mean?

Name _____ Date _____

ASSIGNMENT: Name-Calling, Glittering Generalities

1. Study the advertisements in your local newspaper. How many glittering generalities can you find? Give some examples. _____

_____

_____

_____

_____

2. Can you find any examples of name-calling or use of scary language? _____

_____

_____

_____

_____

3. You are running for dogcatcher of the town of Prairie View. Your opponent, Mr. Cato Ketchem, is ahead of you in the polls. Write a campaign speech for yourself, calling as many names and using as many glittering generalities as possible. _____

_____

_____

_____

_____

_____

_____

_____

PART FIVE: PROPAGANDA

30. Plain Folks on the Bandwagon

Most of us have mixed feelings about our leaders. On one hand, we want them to be better people than we are—stronger, smarter, wiser. When we elect a person President, we devoutly hope he is more intelligent than we are, more knowledgeable about the world's problems, and better able to solve them. When the President appoints a Secretary of State, it is our sincere wish that she will be more diplomatic than we would be, better acquainted with the different cultures of the world, more determined in the pursuit of peace. When we choose a dogcatcher, we hope he will prove to be braver than we are and better able to subdue and capture an enraged Doberman, but we also hope he will be more compassionate and better able to find good homes for orphan puppies.

At the same time, however, we don't want our leaders to be so far superior that they are incapable of understanding our problems and our daily struggles. Superman from Krypton might be a hero, but he could never be elected President. Yes, we want our leaders to be strong, brave, wise, clever, energetic, dedicated, thrifty, and compassionate—but, oddly enough, we also want them to be ordinary people just like ourselves.

Hence, whenever an election draws near, the typical candidate will grab his fishing pole, call his golden retriever, and head for the trout stream or the family farm to pose for his campaign picture. "I'm just an ordinary small-town guy," he will say, or "I'm just an old country lawyer," or "I'm really just a simple farmer." He is using the effective and reassuring **plain folks** propaganda device.

Plain folks appeal is often deceptive: some of these "old country lawyers" and "simple farmers" have millions of dollars in the bank. Besides, the folksiness of a candidate is far less important than his experience, his character, his ideas, and his good judgment. A wise citizen will not let his heart be unduly warmed by a candidate's claim that he is just "an ordinary guy."

Equally popular is the **bandwagon** device, a great favorite of advertisers as well as politicians. You've seen the device many times on television: a screen filled with dancing people, parades, cheering crowds, and a slogan: *Join the New Generation—Eat Crunchmore Breakfast Cereal* or *Foghorn! the People's Choice for the U.S. Senate.* The theme of the bandwagon device is simple: "Everybody's doing it; join the crowd; don't be left out"—a powerful appeal, because all of us want to fit in, and few people want to be considered old-fashioned, slow to catch on, behind the times, or out of the mainstream. But before we rush off to join "everybody" and buy a year's supply of Crunchmore Cereal or vote for Foghorn, we should remember our grandmothers' words of wisdom: "And if 'everybody' were jumping off a cliff—would it be a good idea for you to jump off a cliff too?" We should also remember that Adolph Hitler, one of the most cruel dictators in history, once enjoyed widespread popular support. Popularity is no guarantee of wisdom or goodness.

The opposite of the bandwagon device might be called **snob appeal,** which is not widely popular among politicians, but occasionally used by advertisers: "Crunchmore Cereal is not for everyone. Our sophisticated blend of wholesome grains and delectable honey is only for special people with discriminating tastes—people like you!" Again the appeal is simple: "Be special; be different; don't get lost in the crowd; be an individual—use our product." This device often works because there's a little bit of the snob in all of us, and it certainly would be wonderful if each of us could become special just by eating a breakfast cereal. Again, before we buy, we should ask ourselves a few simple questions: Do I really need this product? Is it worth the cost? Aside from the snob appeal, is it really any better than similar products on the market? It is important to use your own mind and not be distracted by propaganda appeals.

Name _____ Date _____

ASSIGNMENT: More Propaganda Devices

1. Can you think of any historical figures who were not particularly folksy, but who were nevertheless effective leaders? _____

_____

2. Have you ever bought a product or taken some action because "everybody was doing it," only to find later that you had made a mistake?_____

_____

_____

3. What is a snob? Can you think of any particular products that have snob appeal?

_____

_____

4. Using the bandwagon device, write an advertisement for Fizzle Cola.

_____

_____

_____

_____

5. Using snob appeal, write an advertisement for Cloud Nine Sportswear.

_____

_____

_____

_____

_____

PART FIVE: PROPAGANDA

31. The Transfer: "My Opponent Looks Like Hitler!"

The **transfer** device is also called *guilt or glory by association.* In order to use this device, the propagandist invokes the names of people or institutions that most of us love, respect, and revere. He then attempts to *transfer* these positive feelings to himself or to some project he supports. Thus, when Senator Foghorn announces he will seek re-election, he stands before a screen that displays huge pictures of George Washington, Abraham Lincoln, Theodore Roosevelt, John Kennedy, and Martin Luther King, Jr. He sprinkles his speech with quotations from these famous men (but he gets some of the quotations wrong). He also takes care to mention that his father was an Eagle Scout, his mother was a lifelong member of the Daughters of the American Revolution, and he, himself, is a devoted fan of the Chicago Bulls.

Now it may well be true that Senator Foghorn doesn't know Lincoln from Roosevelt, that he was never a Boy Scout, that he confuses the Revolutionary War with the War of 1812, and that he could not make a free throw if his life depended upon it. Foghorn hopes the voters will never stop to consider these possibilities. He knows most Americans have positive feelings about Washington, Lincoln, Roosevelt, Kennedy, King, the Boy Scouts of America, the American Revolution, and the Chicago Bulls. He wants to *transfer* those good feelings to himself.

Senator Foghorn can also use this device in reverse. "My opponent has a mustache just like Hitler's," he will say, or "My opponent was born and raised in Snake County, an area that is notorious for its active chapter of the American Nazi Party." Now if Foghorn's opponent were really a member of the Nazi Party and he kept a portrait of Hitler on his desk, Foghorn would have a right and even a duty to warn the public. Chances are, however, that the opponent has nothing in common with the Nazis except for his Hitler-style mustache. Furthermore, Snake County might be equally famous for its annual antique car show and quilting fair. But Foghorn never mentions these possibilities. He wants his audience to react in fear to those dreaded names *Hitler* and *Nazi.*

Foghorn's constituents should listen with an open mind. They should say to themselves, "Well, the Senator gives a good speech, but what was his actual record in the Boy Scouts? And did George Washington really say, 'Ask what your country can do for you'?"

Name _____ Date _____

ASSIGNMENT: Glory or Guilt by Association

1. List the names of some people (living or dead) who are loved and respected by most people today.

Mother Teresa, _____

_____

2. Now list the names of people who are widely feared or hated.

Benedict Arnold, _____

_____

3. Can you think of any fictional characters whose names might be used in the transfer device?

King Arthur, Count Dracula, _____

_____

4. List some organizations that are admired by most people. _____

_____

5. List some organizations that are feared by many people. _____

_____

Read the following campaign speech and fill in the blank spaces with names of your choice:

My fellow citizens, I promise that if I am elected President, I will be a leader in the tradition of great American men and women such as _____ , _____ , and _____ . I was raised to believe in the grand traditions and lofty ideals of that great organization, _____ . Furthermore, in my beloved home town, the local _____ was always a strong presence. From earliest childhood, I have cherished all that is right and good. But how can anyone seriously consider voting for my opponent? He reminds everyone of _____ . He has a face like _____ and a voice like _____ . Furthermore, it is a well-known fact that his great-grandfather was a member of _____ . Obviously, my opponent is a dangerous man.

PART FIVE: PROPAGANDA

32. Argument to the Man; Argument to the People

The Latin phrase *argumentum ad hominem* means "argument to the man." Usually this device takes the form of an irrelevant personal attack: "My opponent walks like an arthritic giraffe, and his voice sounds like the honking of a flu-stricken goose. He comes to meetings wearing clothes that were rejected by the Salvation Army. And what of his personal life? He is divorced from his first wife, and his present wife wears a rag-mop hairdo and spends thousands of dollars each year on clothes and jewelry. And as if that weren't bad enough, his oldest brother is a drunkard and his youngest brother recently had a nervous breakdown."

Granted, it would be nice to have leaders who looked like Greek gods, who had impeccable taste in clothes, and who came from perfect all-American families. But such personal matters have little to do with a candidate's ability to hold office. Personal matters have even less to do with scientific discovery. Dr. Frankenstein might be as ugly as a gargoyle; he might have been married ten times; he might have five brothers and twenty cousins in the state penitentiary; but if you were suffering from a rare and fatal disease, and if Dr. Frankenstein had discovered a cure, you would probably accept his treatment with joy, forgetting all about his strange appearance and unfortunate family. If Dr. Frankenstein says that the sky is blue, and if he is correct, all the persona attacks in the world will not turn the sky green.

Of course, personal information is sometimes important. If a candidate has had twenty nervous breakdowns, he would probably be a poor choice for a highly stressful position such as President of the United States. If Dr. Frankenstein has a history of poisoning his patients, you would naturally avoid him in spite of his brilliance. More often, however, the *ad hominem* attack is nothing but a propaganda device, designed to mislead.

Another Latin phrase, *argumentum ad populum,* means "argument to the people." This device is easy to use and guaranteed to be popular: the propagandist simply goes around *telling people how wonderful they are.* Senator Foghorn uses this method when he makes a speech at the local high school. "It is so wonderful to be here with you young people—idealistic, energetic, the hope and future of the world!" Later that same day, of course, he may give another speech at the retirement center: "How glad I am to be here with you senior citizens! Your hard work built and sustained this country, and only your wisdom and experience can keep us on our true and proper course." Everyone loves to bask in the rosy warmth of praise—and there's no harm in doing so once in a while, as long as we don't become so happy that we forget about the issues.

65

Name _____ Date _____

ASSIGNMENT: Propaganda Devices

Identify the following propaganda devices:

1. Join the millions of satisfied customers who shop at Save-Mart! _____

_____

2. My opponent has an ape-like face that could crack mirrors and a high-pitched voice that shatters glass! _____

_____

3. I, Congressman Megabucks, am really just a plain, ordinary, hard-working, taxpaying citizen like everyone else. _____

_____

4. I'm opposed to the mayor's wild-eyed socialist scheme to build a new bridge across the Skunk River. _____

_____

5. As your representative to the state legislature, I always enjoy my visits with the warm, friendly, wonderful people of Prairie View._____

_____

6. Vote for Foghorn, a candidate who still believes in hard work, decency, family values, and the American dream. _____

_____

7. Wise old Benjamin Franklin said, " A penny saved is a penny earned," and I agree with him. That's why I'd make a good treasurer of the freshman class. _____

_____

8. Dare to be different—to be original—to be as special as you really are! Smacko Chewing Gum will give your mouth an individualistic flair. _____

_____

9. I'm opposed to the mayor's ridiculous scheme to build a new bridge across the Skunk River—an idea worthy of the Ku Klux Klan. _____

_____

10. Dine with the rich and famous at Rene's French Bistro, where only the most costly food and drink are served. Space is limited. Make your reservation today! _____

_____

PART FIVE: PROPAGANDA

33. The Testimonial

If you have ever watched television, you are familiar with the device of the **testimonial.** A famous movie star appears on your TV screen. She is wearing casual but fashionable clothes and is seated at a well-appointed breakfast table, which for some reason has been placed on the porch of a white farmhouse. Flowers blossom in the yard beyond the porch railing; the morning sun shines; birds sing from the treetops. "I'm Gloria Van Google," she says with an engaging smile. "When I'm filming on location, I need a lot of energy to get me through my demanding day. So I start every morning off right with a nutritious breakfast of Crunchmore Cereal."

You change to another channel and hear a different message. "You know me as Cliff Dunkitt, famous basketball star," a young man says earnestly, "but I'm also an American citizen who is concerned about the future of the country. That's why I'm supporting the re-election of Congressman Megabucks, a proven leader."

A *testimonial* is a statement of support from a well-liked public figure—often an athlete or a film star. The problem with this device should be obvious: Cliff Dunkitt may be a great basketball star and a charming man, and he may be sincere in his support of Congressman Megabucks, but he probably doesn't know any more about politics than the average citizen. Gloria Van Google may or may not be a great actress, but how could she possibly be qualified to give advice about nutrition? How much money is she being paid to endorse Crunchmore Cereal, and is she really an unbiased witness? (A farm? As far as anyone knows, she's lived in Hollywood since she was two years old; why is she posing as a farmer's daughter? And how many farmers eat a late, leisurely breakfast on the front porch, at a table set with a linen cloth, fine china, and sterling silverware?)

If you like, enjoy Ms. Van Google's films and Mr. Dunkitt's heroics on the basketball court—but if you need advice about nutrition or politics, you would do better to consult a reputable doctor or the editorial page of a good newspaper.

Name _____ Date _____

ASSIGNMENT: Propaganda Devices

Can you identify the propaganda devices in the following speech? What kind of information is surprisingly missing?

My friends and fellow citizens, I'm here this afternoon to tell you why you should elect me, Cato Ketchem, as dogcatcher of Prairie View. First of all, let me say once again what I've said so many times in the past: the people of Prairie View are the kindest, friendliest, most hard-working people in the country, and I'm proud to be one of you—a loyal son of rural America, the world of Thomas Jefferson and Abraham Lincoln. I'm proud of our local 4-H organization and everything it stands for. Let me state my position firmly and without eqivocation: I believe in the time-honored values of small-town America, and I believe every American boy and girl deserves a loving family, complete with a devoted pet.

My opponent may appear to be a man of good intentions, but he is well-known as a reckless big-spender and an impractical dreamer. He combines the shrewd sense of Don Quixote, the maturity of Peter Pan, and the rugged good looks of the Scarecrow of Oz. And consider his background: His father lost all of the family's money by investing in a ridiculous scheme to build and sell computerized toe nail clippers, and his mother—a woman who looks exactly like Cruella DeVille—is a lunatic who believes she is a reincarnation of the famous outlaw, Belle Starr. Besides, my opponent is a native of the city of Urbanopolis, a place of crime-torn streets and corrupt big business. On the other hand, my candidacy has been endorsed by Cliff Dunkitt, a brilliant example of a local boy who lived the American dream and became a famous basketball star. More and more citizens of Prairie View have joined Cliff and expressed their support. So remember: A vote for Cato Ketchem is a vote for the good of Prairie View.

_____

_____

_____

_____

_____

_____

_____

_____

_____

_____

_____

PART FIVE: PROPAGANDA

34. Doublespeak, Gobbledygook, and Weasel Words

The term **doublespeak** refers to misleading language, words that are deliberately intended to deceive people or confuse them. In the modern world, doublespeak often takes the form of **gobbledygook,** a long-winded, pretentious, pompous sort of language that is dearly loved by lawyers, government workers, and (unfortunately) some scholars and teachers. In fact, gobbledygook is the favorite language of show-offs everywhere, because it makes them sound much smarter, much better-educated, and much more knowledgeable than they really are.

Gobbledygook may sound intimidating, but it is actually quite easy to write. With a little practice, you can do it too. Here are a few simple guidelines: (1) Use vague nouns, as many as possible, and the bigger the better. Words like *factor, feature, model, module, concept,* and *case* are good, but if you want to sound really impressive and confusing, throw in a few *parameters, objectives, interfaces, contingencies, hegemonies,* and *transmogrifications.* You don't have to worry about what the words mean, because nobody is going to understand you anyway. (2) Avoid adjectives whenever possible; use nouns to modify other nouns, as in *student stratification scale, maturation guidance module,* or *feasibility hypotheses orientation.* (3) If you must use an adjective, pick a big fuzzy one like *environmental, sufficient, sequential,* or *interdependent.* Adjectives that end in *ized* are usually good: *systematized, optimized,* or *individualized,* as in *systematized total education concept* or *individualized creativity module.* (4) This next rule is most important: **Avoid interesting verbs.** Instead use either the passive voice or the verb *be* in every sentence if possible. Or look for verbs that end in *ize: marginalize, socialize, synchronize, revitalize, demonize, stigmatize.*

Follow these rules carefully, and you will be able to speak and write so learnedly that everyone will be in awe of you—and it won't matter whether you are telling the truth or not, because nothing you say will make any sense. Translated into gobbledygook, Julius Caesar's famous statement, "I came; I saw; I conquered," might have come out like this:

A lateralized strategic approach was conducted; and, after the contiguous terrain was subjected to a cursory sequentialized orientation study, optimized assertive maneuvers were conducted with maximum efficiency, resulting in immediate subjugation ascendancy.

Advertisers use gobbledygook occasionally ("If you're *aspirin-allergic,* try *doctor-recommended* Head-eeze!"), but their preferred form of doublespeak is a misleading little **weasel word** such as *helps, works, fights, can be,* or *virtually.* "Head-eeze *helps* ease the ache and fever of the common cold." "Silkentress Shampoo *virtually* eliminates dandruff!" "Hercules Bathroom Cleaner *fights* to dissolve grime and kill germs." "Foamwell Toothpaste *works* to control tooth decay and *can be* effective against bad breath." At first glance, the makers of these products appear to promise wonderful things—no more headaches, dandruff, tooth decay, bad breath, or germ-infested grime. But the beauty of a weasel word is that it seems to make promises without actually doing so. The makers of Head-eeze don't

69

really say their medicine will *cure* a headache, only that it will *help* ease the pain. (Time and Mother Nature will have to do the rest of the work.) Hercules Cleanser may well *fight* against grime and germs, but does it ever win those battles? Nobody is saying. What does it mean to be *virtually* free of dandruff? The advantage of a weasel word is that it doesn't mean much of anything.

Name _____ Date _____

ASSIGNMENT: Write Your Own Propaganda

Now that you have studied the propaganda devices, the time has come for you to try your own wings as a propagandist.

1. Choose a product—real or fictitious—that you would like to advertise: _____

_____

_____

2. Write an advertisement for this product, using as many propaganda devices and weasel words as possible: _____

_____

_____

_____

_____

_____

_____

_____

_____

_____

_____

_____

3. On your own paper, write a campaign speech for Congressman Megabucks. Use the plain folks device, the bandwagon device, the post hoc fallacy, argument to the man, argument to the people, and any other device or fallacy you like.

PART SIX: THE CREATIVE PROCESS

35. Eureka! Preparation and Illumination

We hear a lot about "creativity" these days. Students are constantly told to "be creative" in their schoolwork and even in their play. Teachers talk about "the creative process," and people in business look for "creative" solutions to their problems. Classes in "creative writing" abound. But what, exactly, is "the creative process"? Does such a thing really exist, or is the phrase just another glittering generality?

The answer is yes, the human mind actually does perform according to a "creative process" (also known as "problem solving"). Furthermore, psychologists have studied this process and identified four distinct stages. Using this method, the human mind can combine old pieces of information into something completely new—a new invention, new knowledge about the universe, a work of art that is unlike anything ever seen before.

The first stage is called **preparation.** This stage is a time of careful study or research. The problem-solver studies his problem in as much detail as possible. He reads books, talks to people, and observes the situation. If he is a detective trying to solve a murder, for example, he has already done a good deal of preparation before he ever takes the case. He knows about poisons, weapons, criminal motives, and the law; he learned these things when he went to school. And after he makes up his mind to solve the mystery, he has to do further preparation—examine the evidence, talk to the suspects, and visit the scene of the crime. He may have to walk a good many miles before he is ready to announce his solution.

In fact, he may walk so many miles, talk to so many people, and squint at so many bits of broken glass and globs of caked blood that his feet get sore, his voice grows hoarse, and his head aches. At some point, he will probably have to take a rest and think about something else—anything else except his case. So he puts his work aside and goes to a concert, takes a swim in the ocean, brushes his dog's fur, or lies down for a nap. This stage is known as **incubation,** a period of purposeful relaxation. To some impatient people, this step might look like a waste of time, because the detective now appears to have lost all interest in solving the mystery.

His mind is never entirely still, however. While he is swimming or listening to music, his subconscious mind continues to sift through the evidence, trying to combine the pieces of the puzzle into a unified whole. One day, maybe when he least expects it—while he is taking a shower, walking his dog, or making an omelet—the pieces come together, and he knows the solution to the mystery—or at least he has reached a new stage in the investigation. He thinks of something that has never occurred to him before, and this new idea is the key to the problem. Fittingly, this stage is called **illumination.**

It would be nice if the detective could stop here, announce his conclusion, collect his fee, and have his picture taken for the newspapers. But he's not finished yet. His brilliant idea won't mean much to a judge and jury unless he can prove his case with evidence. So back to work he goes, taking a fresh look at the evidence to make certain his flash of inspiration was the real thing, not just an idle dream. This final stage is called **verification.** If the evidence really fits as expected, the detective can now confidently announce the identity of the murderer, and the police can make an arrest.

It is important to note that **not one of the four steps can work by itself.** Hard work and careful study are effective only up to a point: endless *preparation* never solved a problem or provided the basis for a satisfying life. *Incubation,* to some people, is the most attractive part of the process—just lie back, relax, and let the good ideas flow! But to incubate an empty mind is like expecting birds to hatch out of thin air. It is impossible to have brilliant ideas about nothing. A prepared, relaxed mind is most likely to provide *illumination.* However, the light of illumination can be unconvincing or misleading unless the thinker is willing to provide *verification.*

Name _____ Date _____

ASSIGNMENT: The Creative Process

In the following short story, a pair of young detectives must use their creative minds in order to solve a baffling puzzle. Read "The Mystery of the Lost Letter" and try to identify the stages in the creative process:

1. In what ways do Annie and Kevin **prepare** to solve the mystery? _____

_____

_____

_____

2. Why are they temporarily forced to abandon their search for the lost letter? _____

_____

_____

_____

3. At what point does the **illumination** occur? _____

_____

_____

4. In what way does Annie **verify** her idea? _____

_____

_____

5. Why do Kevin and Annie make a good team? _____

_____

_____

_____

PART SIX: THE CREATIVE PROCESS

36. Short Story: The Mystery of the Lost Letter

"Exactly what did Grammy write in her diary?" Annie asked her twin brother, Kevin.

"Just that she was cleaning out her grandfather's desk and found a letter signed 'A. Lincoln.'" He read aloud from the tattered red diary: "I can't believe this is a real letter from Abraham Lincoln, because the penmanship is even worse than mine. But just in case, to keep the letter from getting lost or stolen, I've put it in the box with the wedding rings."

Annie glanced around the living room of the fine old lakeside home that had once belonged to her grandmother, the house where the family would be staying for the summer. Her eyes rested on the secretary where Kevin had found the diary. The old desk was packed with books and bulging with old papers.

"Didn't Lincoln usually sign his letters 'A. Lincoln' instead of 'Abraham'?" she asked. "And didn't he write with a scribble?"

"That's what Mr. Grant said in history class last year!" Kevin sounded excited. "If we could find that letter, we'd be guaranteed to win first prize at the History Fair next year, and we'd probably get an A in history, too."

Annie ran her fingers through her hair as she thought aloud. "Grammy said she put the letter in a box with some wedding rings. That means a jewelry box."

"I'll bet it's in the attic!" Kevin said, jumping to his feet. "History Fair, here we come."

The attic was a pile of boxes, trunks, old books, toys, worn-out board games, and suitcases. "So many boxes!" Annie said. She opened a hat box and found a black velvet hat with a broad brim and a long feather. She ran her finger along the feather and then set the hat on the floor, planning to try it on later. She opened a bread box, which turned out to be jammed with doll clothes.

Kevin sneezed as he opened a large chest. "Nothing here but some old quilts," he said. "Have you found a jewelry box?"

Annie was standing on a chair to reach the top shelf of the closet. "Yes, a big one. Come help me!"

They got the box down, opened it, and began taking out costume jewelry—cameo pins, brooches in the shapes of owls and elephants, clattering necklaces that were heavy with artificial rubies and diamonds. At the end of a long chain, a golden peacock spread its jeweled tail. Annie slipped the chain around her neck and held an owl-shaped pin against her sweater.

"Too bad these jewels aren't real," Kevin said. "We could buy the school and give ourselves an A in history." He shrugged. "Well, no sign of a letter from Lincoln or anyone else. Want to try the basement?"

In the basement, they found a trunk full of old clothes, a box of buttons and thread, and a chest of tools, but no jewelry boxes. "What about the desk?" Annie said. She started taking books out of the drawers. "Look! Grammy's old Girl Scout Handbook and her school books! Grammy never threw a book away, did she?" Then her hands touched a box. "Kevin, I think I've found it!" Kevin grinned at his sister as she drew out a small wooden box, beautifully painted with blue and white flowers. It was the right shape to hold a letter.

73

Annie opened it carefully. Tissue paper was folded inside. "I think there's some kind of jewelry in here," she said. "Something round and gold—"

"Wow! Granddad's gold watch!" Kevin exclaimed. "It's been lost for years!"

The twins looked at each other. "Well," said Annie, "we've found the watch, which will make Mom and Dad happy, and we've found enough stuff to open our own antique shop."

"If we want an A in history, I guess we'll have to get it the old-fashioned way—study," Kevin said. "But I think we must be forgetting something. Look, we didn't know Grammy very well, but we do know she was smart, right?"

"Dad says she was the smartest person he knew."

"She wanted to hide the letter where it wouldn't be stolen. Now think: if you were a burglar, where's the first place you'd look for something valuable to steal?"

"In the china cabinet where the silverware is, of course, or in—in a jewelry box."

"Right! Would our brainy grandmother pick such an obvious place to hide a valuable letter?"

"No," Annie admitted. "We've forgotten something, but what?"

Even in the summer, the lakeside house grew cold after dark. That night Annie went upstairs to her room, crawled into bed, and settled underneath her red-and-blue patchwork quilt. She loved the cool nights and the warm bed, but tonight she could not fall asleep. Visions of shiny rings began to swirl in her mind. *Whose wedding rings?* she wondered. *Where would you put a wedding ring except in a jewelry box?* A cool breeze ruffled the curtains, and Annie snuggled under the quilt, enjoying its warmth and softness.

Suddenly she sat up in bed. Wedding rings—quilts—a box! She sprang out of bed and tiptoed to her brother's doorway.

"Kevin? Are you asleep? I think I know where the missing letter is. Didn't you find some old quilts in the attic?"

"Yes, in the big wooden box at the foot of the bed, but—"

"That's where the letter is. Come on."

"But what do quilts have to do with anything?" asked Kevin as he followed his sister upstairs.

"It's what we forgot!" Annie opened the box and unfolded a white quilt that was covered with patches in bright, bold circular patterns. "There's a kind of quilt called a 'wedding ring'! We're going to get that A in history after all—and get our pictures in the paper when we hand this letter over to the museum." Carefully she felt between the folds of the quilts and pulled out a folded piece of yellowed paper.

"The Mystery of the Lost Letter" used by permission of Highlights for Children, Inc., Columbus, Ohio. Copyrighted material.

PART SIX: THE CREATIVE PROCESS

37. Use Your Creative Powers

Real-life detectives rarely work in quite the same way that fictional detectives do. (For one thing, a real detective seldom encounters a mysterious locked room with a corpse cleverly hidden inside, and it isn't often that he finds a whole cast of suspects conveniently staying in the same creaky old mansion.) Nevertheless, the mystery story offers a useful illustration of how the mind works to solve problems. In "The Mystery of the Lost Letter," Kevin and Annie learn that a valuable document—a letter in Abraham Lincoln's handwriting—is hidden somewhere in the house that once belonged to their grandmother. If the twins can find the letter, they are all but guaranteed to have a prize-winning entry in the History Fair—but where is the mysterious "box with the wedding rings" where the letter is supposed to be hidden?

Kevin and Annie begin by making a complete search of the attic and the basement. Before they are finished, they have opened every box they can find, but none of the many boxes contain an old letter. The twins' time of preparation ends when both Annie and Kevin have run out of ideas. Neither can think of any more places to search; Kevin is convinced they are overlooking an important clue, but he has no notion of what that clue might be.

That night Annie snuggles in bed and allows her mind to wander. She thinks of rings, boxes, and quilts. This is her time of incubation. Visions of brightly-colored rings begin to dance before her mind's eye—and suddenly she experiences a moment of illumination. She realizes the "box" is actually a cedar chest, and the "wedding rings" are not pieces of jewelry, but quilts made with circular patterns.

Now that Annie has solved the mystery, why doesn't she immediately call her history teacher, Mr. Grant, and tell him about the wonderful prize-winning project for the History Fair? Obviously, because she would look foolish if her idea turned out to be wrong. She and Kevin are not going to say anything about their discovery until they have verified it by searching the cedar chest and actually examining the letter from Abraham Lincoln.

Kevin and Annie make a good team of detectives because their minds work differently. In some ways, Kevin is better at preparation than his sister is. After all, it was Kevin's idea to go rummaging through the old secretary and start reading the family papers. Kevin is quicker to think of places to search for the letter, and he is the first to realize that a jewelry box is exactly the *wrong* place to look—their grandmother was too clever to hide the letter in such an obvious place. But Annie, the more thoughtful of the twins, is the one who provides the flash of illumination necessary to solve the mystery. Neither could have found the lost letter without the other's help.

Can the average person learn to be a creative thinker? Certainly we can't all compose symphonies, solve crimes, or discover new planets. But we can use our minds more effectively if we always remember what we know about the creative process.

How can you cultivate your creative powers? First of all, don't neglect preparation. Don't get the idea that you can simply "be creative" without learning any information. Instead, be a good student—not just in one subject, but in as many subjects as possible. Read your assignments, do your homework, and learn the facts. If possible, sign up for a class in psychology and learn something about people and why they behave as they do. Start reading the newspapers or watching newscasts and find out what's going on in your home town, in your country, and in the world.

But preparation is more than study and reading; you will also prepare your mind by joining organizations or participating in music or sports. Travel is excellent preparation for creativity. If you can't go to Paris, San Francisco, or Hawaii, then travel to the nearest state park or to the next town. And when you reach your destination, observe as much as possible. You might be surprised at what you can learn just by going to a place that's a little bit different, a little bit unfamiliar.

Work hard, but don't wear yourself out. Both your mind and your body need to rest occasionally. If you want to be creative, it is important for you to get enough sleep and take some time to relax. Exercise and good food will also help; your mind will be more alert if your body is healthy and strong. If you don't care for sports, then at least turn off the television set, shut down the computer, and get out of the house occasionally. Take your dog for a walk, or stroll beside the lake and watch the sun set. Ride a horse, go for a swim, or climb the stairs instead of taking the elevator. And sometimes you need to spend a little time just doing nothing. Don't fill your schedule with so many activities that you hardly have time to breathe.

The light of illumination will shine best in an open mind. If you want to be creative, become interested in as many different subjects as possible. Try a new activity or hobby occasionally, and talk with people whose experiences are different from your own. Listen to different styles of music; learn a foreign language; study the life and culture of a foreign country. Learn to appreciate people for what they are instead of expecting them to be perfect. Learn not to get upset when somebody disagrees with you or questions your ideas.

How are you at verification? Do you submit sloppy, half-finished homework without taking time to revise or to check your facts? If so, resolve to mend your ways. Look at your homework a second time before you prepare a finished copy to give the teacher. If you are unsure of your facts, don't guess—go to the library and look up the information you need. Never confuse creativity with laziness.

Following this plan will not necessarily make you a genius or earn you a million dollars. You may not win the Nobel Prize, get elected president, or even get A's on your homework. But you will have the satisfaction of using your mind to its best possible advantage—and, incidentally, you may also find yourself living a healthy, happy, interesting life.